THE ENTREPRENEURS'

COMPANION

A USEFUL REFERENCE BOOK FOR
DECISION-MAKERS IN BUSINESS

ELIJAH M. JAMES, PH.D.

Canadian Cataloging in Publication Data
James, Elijah M.
The Entrepreneurs' Companion

ISBN 978-1-7383576-8-0

EJ Publishing
663 White Plains Run
Hammonds Plains
Nova Scotia, Canada B4B 1W7

This book is dedicated to the late Dr. Evelyn Weekes, a friend and colleague who epitomized the spirit of entrepreneurship.

Table of Contents

PREFACE

When I was a teenager, I owned a book called *The Students' Companion* written by Wilfred D. Best. It was loaded with general knowledge. In my circle of friends at that time, it was a severe disadvantage not to have access to a copy of that book if you were a serious student. Generations of students through the years benefited from that book. Even as an adult, I have often referred to *The Students' Companion* for information on various topics. It was truly, the students' companion.

There is no shortage of excellent books on various aspects of business ownership and management. However, this author is not aware of any book that will be to entrepreneurs and businesspersons what the Students' Companion has been to students over the years. The Entrepreneurs' Companion is intended to fill that gap.

What exactly is The Entrepreneurs' Companion? Let us answer the question by stating what it is not. The Entrepreneurs' Companion is not a typical textbook with learning exercises and other pedagogical devices such as one would use in business textbooks, although it is expected that one will learn from it. Neither is it a glossary of business terms, although one will certainly learn many business concepts from it, and the book does contain a Glossary at the end. Instead, it is a book with useful information to help entrepreneurs understand many aspects of business operations and make sound business decisions.

The Entrepreneurs' Companion dispenses with tedious and technical explanations and relies on simple language and true-to-life examples to convey its message.

Each chapter begins with a short introduction that alerts the reader of the material that will be covered in the chapter. It is believed that by informing entrepreneurs of the sites that they will encounter along the way, they will better enjoy the journey.

In each chapter, you will find two very short "business cases" with answers. The purpose is to demonstrate the practical significance of the material presented. Although the cases are short, they force the entrepreneur to reflect on certain business situations and to clarify his or her thinking on certain issues. The answers provide a means whereby the entrepreneur can evaluate his or her thoughts. All the cases are entirely hypothetical.

CHAPTER 1

THE STARTING LINE

This Photo by Unknown Author is licensed under CC BY-SA

Any runner in a race will tell you that it is crucially important to get a good start. For an entrepreneur, a good start is knowing what it takes to be a good entrepreneur.

Introduction

Whoever desires the position of an entrepreneur desires a good thing, but not always. There are advantages and disadvantages to being an entrepreneur. However, before we go any further, let us determine who is an entrepreneur. We will then identify the characteristics of an entrepreneur so that you can decide if you have what it takes to become one. We will end the chapter with a discussion of the advantages and disadvantages of entrepreneurship.

Definition of Entrepreneur

An entrepreneur is someone who organizes natural resources, human resources, and capital resources into the production of goods and services with the expectation of making a profit. Since profits are not guaranteed, the entrepreneur bears the risks involved in his or her undertaking. That is why an entrepreneur is regarded as a risk-taker.

Types of Entrepreneurs

Not all entrepreneurs are created equal. It is important to know what type of entrepreneur you are because it will help you to understand why you make certain business decisions, and what types of businesses you are likely to undertake. Here, we will consider four types of entrepreneurs: the waiting, the conservative, the aggressive, and the innovative. We will deal with each type in turn.

The waiting type Entrepreneurs of this persuasion simply sit and wait for business opportunities to come their way. No one will label them "go-getters". They do not go out of their way to make things happen, but they are ready to seize opportunities that come their way.

The conservative type Entrepreneurs of this ilk are not as laid back as the waiting type. They passively pursue business opportunities and will exert energy and effort to protect their assets. They are willing to assume low risks but unwilling to assume high risks.

The aggressive type Aggressive entrepreneurs are opportunity seekers. Unlike the waiting type, they aggressively seek out business opportunities. They seem to embrace the motto, "Where there's a will there's a way." Aggressive entrepreneurs are willing to engage in high-risk businesses in search of high profits.

The innovative type These types of entrepreneurs rely on their creativity and imaginative ability to make money. They are the entrepreneurs who are considered trailblazers, pioneers, originators, and groundbreakers. They use their innovative skills to create new lines of business. They often come up with new products and services.

Characteristics of Successful Entrepreneurs

Successful entrepreneurs have certain characteristics. They include:

Perseverance

Successful entrepreneurs must be importunate. If, at the first sign of difficulty, you decide to shut up shop, then you are unlikely to succeed as an entrepreneur. Successful entrepreneurs are persistent. They know that in order to succeed, sometimes you have to try, try, and try again. This does not suggest that successful entrepreneurs are foolhardy. They know when an idea is just not worth pursuing further.

Perceptiveness

Perceptiveness is the ability to perceive things or ideas quickly, the ability to quickly see through things that are not immediately obvious. This quality in entrepreneurs enables them to see the wisdom of undertaking a business venture while others are still lingering in the valley of decision.

Self-motivation

Self-motivation can be considered as the force within you that propels you into action. It brings out the positivity in you that tells to that you can do it. Entrepreneurs who lack self-motivation have little or no incentive to get up and go. They may have dreams but have no motivation to follow their dreams. This is hardly a recipe for success.

Networking ability

Success as an entrepreneur requires the ability to interact with many different kinds of people. Entrepreneurs need to be in contact with and develop relationships with suppliers, customers, community leaders, and others with whom they can form partnerships. These partnerships are often critical to business success.

Passion

If you are passionate about sports, music, health, or education, you will pursue those things actively and without being prompted. Successful entrepreneurs are passionate about their businesses. They wake up in the mornings with the business on their minds and they fall asleep at nights with the business on their minds. It is passion that enables entrepreneurs to invest time, effort, energy, and other resources to ensure business success.

Optimism

Optimism is the tendency to see the positive and bright side of things. Optimism allows entrepreneurs to be hopeful even when situations are less than ideal. Because of optimism, they plod onward under less-than-favorable circumstances.

Risk-taking

By definition, entrepreneurs are risk-takers. They spend money on business ventures, without any guarantee or certainty that they will earn a profit. Yet, they bear the risk. At the heart of the entrepreneurial spirit is risk-taking. It is that more than anything else that identifies entrepreneurs. If you are not a risk-taker, you are unlikely to be involved in business ventures that make significant profits.

Goal orientation

Another important characteristic of successful entrepreneurs is the ability to set goals and work towards achieving them. Goals give you focus, commitment, and direction as they give you something to aim for. An aimless business person does not have a set target and is unlikely to find success in business.

Ability to persuade

The ability to persuade and convince others is an important characteristic of successful entrepreneurs. Entrepreneurship often requires the ability to accomplish tasks by giving instructions to others. Other things being equal, the greater the ability to persuade and convince, the more successful will be the entrepreneur.

Creativity

Creativity is the ability that enables an individual to come up with new ideas and new ways of doing things. It is the heart of innovation. Entrepreneurs with creativity will be a step or two ahead of the pack. Businesses face a variety of problems. Creativity gives the entrepreneur the edge in finding creative solutions to problems.

Knowledge

Sir Francis Bacon correctly said that "knowledge itself is power." Successful entrepreneurs must be knowledgeable about many things. Although complete knowledge is beyond the realm of entrepreneurs, they should possess much knowledge about their products/services, their customers, the markets they serve, and the environment in which they operate. Change is constantly occurring, and in order to be successful, entrepreneurs must keep abreast of developments in their industry.

BUSINESS CASE 1.1

Desmond is an excellent cook. He worked as a chef at a restaurant where he delighted many customers with his culinary skills. On his way home from work, he saw a "FOR RENT" sign on a building. "That would be great for a restaurant", he thought. Filled with excitement, he convinced his wife that they should start their own business as restaurateurs because everyone loves his cooking.

What important fact might Desmond be overlooking?

Answer

The ability to cook well is certainly a desirable quality for a restaurant operator to possess, but it is not the only characteristic for success as an entrepreneur. Desmond might be overlooking that fact. The successful operation of a restaurant requires other skills and qualities such as insight, decision-making skills, the ability to communicate well, creativity, and self-motivation.

Advantages of Entrepreneurship

Entrepreneurship has benefits for entrepreneurs as well as for the economy. Let us first consider the advantages for entrepreneurs.

Advantages for entrepreneurs

Potential for high income One of the advantages of entrepreneurship is the potential to earn excessively large income in the form of profits. If entrepreneurs work hard, make good business decisions, and are willing to assume high risks, they stand to make huge profits.

Freedom of choice with respect to work Entrepreneurship gives you the opportunity to decide, within limits, when you want to work. Whereas most employees have scheduled working hours, that is not the case with entrepreneurs. They have the luxury of choosing when they want to work.

Pride of business ownership Business ownership confers a certain amount of pride on entrepreneurs. This is evidenced by the proud manner in which entrepreneurs announce: "I own my own business." The independence associated with entrepreneurship is a veritable source of pride.

Relative job security Entrepreneurs have job security for as long as their businesses are in operation. They cannot be fired. This is a tremendous advantage of entrepreneurship and is one of the primary reasons that propel people into becoming entrepreneurs.

Opportunity to make a positive contribution Business ownership gives entrepreneurs the opportunity to make positive impacts on the community in which they operate. Knowing that others benefit from their efforts, entrepreneurs derive satisfaction from their contributions.

Opportunity for growth and development Through the ownership and running of their businesses, entrepreneurs have many opportunities to learn new things and experiment with new ideas. They are often forced to make certain decisions the outcome of which can be important lessons. Running a business often reveals certain deficiencies that entrepreneurs will try to remedy thus leading to personal growth and development.

Possibility of meeting and interacting with business leaders Owning and running their own businesses give entrepreneurs the chance to meet business leaders. They may be actual or potential suppliers or just important contacts. Alliance with these people could enhance business success.

Advantages for the Economy

In the previous section, we considered the advantages of entrepreneurship for entrepreneurs. In this section, we turn our attention to the advantages of entrepreneurship for the economy.

Increase in efficiency In their pursuit of profits, entrepreneurs try to use resources efficiently. They will tend to shift resources from where they are less productive to where they are more productive. In this way, the entire economy benefits as the waste of resources is minimized.

Job creation One occasionally finds an entrepreneur who operates solo. This, however, is not the usual state of affairs. Entrepreneurs generally hire employees to perform a variety of tasks, thus creating employment. For example, a good chef who opens a restaurant employs waiters, waitresses, and other restaurant staff.

Contribution to gross domestic product (GDP) Gross domestic product (GDP) is defined as the market value of all final goods and services produced in an economy during a period of time, usually one year. Consider what would happen to the GDP if all entrepreneurs ceased operation for a week or two.

Creation of new businesses and new products Entrepreneurs create new businesses and new products and services. They identify consumers' needs that are not being adequately met and create businesses to provide goods and services to satisfy those needs.

Increased competition It is generally agreed that competition is good for an economy. Entrepreneurship results in increased competition with its concomitant lower costs, lower prices, and greater output.

Disadvantages of Entrepreneurship

Entrepreneurship is not without its disadvantages. Let us zero in on some of them.

Time requirement Owning and running a business requires a great deal of time on the part of the entrepreneur. It is not a 9 to 5 proposition. As an entrepreneur, you may have to work for extended hours to take care of your business. It is not uncommon for entrepreneurs to begin to work before daybreak and continue to work late into the night.

Unreliable income Regular employees usually have a contract or agreement that allows them to work a certain number of days for a certain amount of money. This is not the case with entrepreneurs. Their incomes are tied to the ups and downs of business. They can earn huge incomes this week, and next to nothing next week.

Stress Entrepreneurship can be very stressful. "Uneasy lies the head that wears the crown" applies in the case of entrepreneurs. Among other things, they worry about inventory, satisfying customers, making good deals with suppliers, and maintaining market shares. The possibility of business failure is hardly ever far from their minds.

Disadvantages for the Economy

The advantages of entrepreneurship for the economy can hardly be denied, but there are disadvantages.

Unwise use of resources Many entrepreneurs start businesses not so much because they are innovative and adventurous, and have the desire to make a meaningful contribution to society, but out of desperation. They lose their jobs, so they start businesses in order to survive. They may not possess any pertinent skills, so their businesses fail and the economy's resources are wasted.

Job loss On the one hand, entrepreneurship creates jobs, but on the other hand, it causes job loss. Entrepreneurs compete with existing firms, taking business away from them, and causing them to lay off workers. Until those laid-off workers find new jobs, they will be unemployed.

BUSINESS CASE 1.2

Paul is a hardworking entrepreneur. His motivation to work hard is due to his belief that the benefits of entrepreneurial activities redound solely to the entrepreneurs. That partly explains the diligence with which they work.

How much credence do you give to Paul's idea that only entrepreneurs benefit from their entrepreneurial activities?

Answer

Paul's idea leaves much to be desired. Surely, entrepreneurs benefit from their activities, and that partly explains their diligence. However, it is worth noting that entrepreneurs are not the only beneficiaries of their activities. Their activities create employment for others, lead to competition and the efficient use of scarce resources, result in the creation and development of new products and services, and contribute to social development.

CHAPTER 2

LEGAL FORMS OF

BUSINESS ORGANIZATION

This Photo by Unknown Author is licensed under CC BY-SA

Many entrepreneurs are single proprietors.

Introduction

It has always been your dream to own your own business, but throughout your life so far, you have always been an employee. You have been frugal and have managed to save $50,000.00. Your present place of employment is downsizing and has decided to offer you a severance package of $30,000.00. This could be your opportunity to own your own business. However, before you begin your journey into becoming a businessperson, there are a few things you need to know, and one of them is the various forms of business organization. In this chapter, we identify the various forms of business organization, point out their advantages and disadvantages, and indicate the factors to consider when choosing a form of business organization.

Forms of Business Organization

An important decision that you will need to make at this early stage is the form of business organization that you should choose for your business. You can choose one of several forms of business organization. Among the most popular, however, are the following:

- The single or sole proprietorship
- The general partnership
- The limited partnership
- The corporation
- The cooperative.

Different countries have different laws about business organization, so what applies in one country may not apply in all.

The various forms of business organization do not merely represent the financial arrangements under which the business operates; they also dictate the extent to which the owners of the business enterprise are liable for the business's debts, which laws will apply to its operation, the owners' role in running the business, and the types of taxes that will be applicable.

The Single Proprietorship

This is the easiest type of business to form. A single proprietorship is a business owned by a single individual who is personally responsible for all debts incurred by the business. So you have decided to use some of your savings along with some of the funds from your severance package to open a small coffee shop. You register your business with the appropriate government authority and presto, you are a business owner. As a single (or sole) proprietor, you own your own business, finance it yourself (perhaps with financial assistance from family and friends), and make all the decisions regarding the operation of your business. If your business succeeds, you enjoy the profits; if it fails, you suffer the losses.

Advantages of the Single Proprietorship

The single proprietorship has several advantages.

1. The single proprietorship is the easiest form of business organization to start. There are few regulatory requirements to meet before establishing a single proprietorship.
2. Single proprietors derive a certain amount of satisfaction, pride, and independence from owning their own businesses. You can sense the feeling of accomplishment when someone proudly announces, "I own my own business."
3. Knowing that they can lose all of their possessions if their businesses fail, single proprietors are likely to make special efforts to run their businesses efficiently.
4. In situations demanding swift action, single proprietorships enjoy a considerable advantage over other forms of business organization, because owners do not need to consult with or seek the agreement of anyone else.

5. Single proprietors are likely to be very concerned about developing good working relations with the few employees that they have and with securing the goodwill of their customers or clients. If single proprietors are successful, the quality of their services will be high and the effect on their revenues favourable.
6. Single proprietors may enjoy tax benefits. The earnings of single proprietors are taxed once only. Corporations do not enjoy this advantage.

Before you jump to the conclusion that the single proprietorship is right for you, let us take a look at some of the disadvantages of that form of business organization.

Disadvantages of the Single Proprietorship

1. Single proprietors are at a distinct disadvantage in situations requiring huge capital outlays. Not many single proprietors are in a position to raise the large sums of money required in some businesses. Hence, we do not find many single proprietors owning large industrial plants.
2. The single proprietorship form of business organization suffers from uncertainty about the continuation of the business in the event of the death or retirement of the owner. However, some single proprietorships have survived through several generations in the hands of the same family.
3. The biggest disadvantage of the single proprietorship is the fact that the owner is legally responsible for all debts of the business. Single proprietors are not protected by limited liability. This means that if their businesses fail, single proprietors are fully liable and can lose personal assets, such as cars, furniture, or even homes, because, in this form of business organization, no legal distinction exists between personal assets and business assets.

Table 2.1 Summary of the Advantages and Disadvantages of the Single Proprietorship

Advantages	Disadvantages
1. Ease of starting	1. Difficulty of raising capital
2. Ownership satisfaction	2. Lack of continuity in the event of death or retirement of owner
3. Incentive for efficiency	3. Owner has unlimited liability
4. Quickness in decision making	
5. Incentive for harmonious work environment	
6. Positive tax benefits	

The Partnership

Here, we will discuss two types of partnerships: the general partnership and the limited partnership. A general partnership is a business owned by two or more people, without limited liability; and a limited partnership is a business owned by two or more people, one or more, but not all, of whom have limited liability.

Let us deal first with the general partnership. Your small coffee shop is doing very well. In fact, business is so good that you can hardly find time to do anything else. You really need help to be able to run the business properly. You discuss the situation with one of your buddies from college who agrees to go into business with you. You draw up a *partnership agreement*, thus forming a general partnership.

A partnership agreement is a legal document that outlines exactly what role the partners will play in the business. It specifies the responsibilities of each partner, how much money each partner contributes to the business, how much of the profits each partner will receive, and how much of the losses will be borne by each partner. The document is typically drawn up by a lawyer and signed by the partners. A sample partnership agreement follows.

A Sample Partnership Agreement

This partnership agreement is made between_____
residing at _____ and _____
residing at _____, (hereafter referred to as the
"Partners").

PARTNERSHIP NAME AND BUSINESS

1. The Partners agree to carry on a business of _____
as partners under the name _____.

No person may be introduced as a Partner and no other business may
be carried on by the Partnership without the consent in writing of the
Partners.

2. The principal place of business of the Partnership is

_____.

TERM

3. The Partnership begins on the _____ day of _____,
20___ and continues until terminated in accordance with this
agreement.

PARTNERSHIP SHARES AND CAPITAL

4. The Partners shall participate in the assets, liabilities, profits, and
losses of the Partnership in the percentages beside their respective
names (their "Partnership Shares"):

_____ (Partner) _____%

_____ (Partner) _____%

_____(Partner) _____%

5. The Partners shall contribute a total of $_____ in cash, in proportion to their respective Partnership Shares, to the start-up capital of the Partnership by no later than the _____ day of _____, 20___.

6. If additional capital is required to carry on the Partnership business, the Partners shall contribute it as required in proportion to their respective Partnership Shares.

7. No interest accrues on a Partner's capital contributions to the Partnership in proportion to his/her Partnership Share. However, if a Partner makes an actual payment or advance for the purpose of the Partnership beyond his/her Partnership Share (an Additional Advance), he/she is entitled to _____% annual interest from the Partnership on the Additional Advance until refunded by the Partnership.

BANKING ARRANGEMENTS AND FINANCIAL RECORDS

8. The Partnership shall maintain a bank account in the name of the Partnership business on which cheques may be drawn only on the signature of at least_____ of the Partners.

9. The Partners shall at all times maintain full and proper accounts of the Partnership business accessible to each of the Partners at any time on reasonable notice.

PARTNERSHIP ACCOUNTS AND SALARIES

10. The financial records of the Partnership shall include separate income and capital accounts for each Partner.

11. No Partner may receive a salary for services rendered to the Partnership but the profit or loss of the Partnership business shall be periodically allocated among the Partners' separate income accounts and each of the Partners may, from time to time, withdraw against a credit balance in his/her income account.

12. The capital accounts of the Partners shall be maintained in proportion to their respective Partnership Shares.

13. No Partner shall draw down his/her capital account without the previous consent in writing of the other Partners. If a Partner draws down his/her capital account below his/her Partnership Share, he/she shall bring it up to his/her Partnership Share on the demand of any of the Partners.

MANAGEMENT OF PARTNERSHIP BUSINESS

14. Each Partner may take part in the management of the Partnership business.

15. Any difference arising in the ordinary course of carrying on the Partnership business shall be decided by the Partners having a majority of the Partnership Shares.

PARTNERSHIP DUTIES AND RESPONSIBILITIES

16. Each Partner shall devote substantially all of his/her ordinary working time to carrying on the business of the Partnership.

17. Each Partner shall at all times duly and punctually pay and discharge his/her separate debts and liabilities and shall save harmless the property of the Partnership and the other Partners from those separate debts and liabilities and, if necessary, shall promptly indemnify the other Partners for their share of any actual payment or discharge of his/her separate debts and liabilities by the Partnership.

18. No Partner shall assign or encumber his/her share or interest in the Partnership without the previous consent in writing of the other Partners.

19. No Partner shall bind the Partnership or the other Partners for anything outside the ordinary course of carrying on the Partnership business.

FISCAL YEAR END

20. The fiscal year end of the Partnership shall be the _____ day of _____ in each year.

TERMINATION OF PARTNERSHIP

21. The Partnership may be dissolved at any time during the joint lives of the Partners by a Partner giving notice in writing to the other Partners of his/her intention to dissolve the Partnership, in which case the Partnership is dissolved as from the date mentioned in the notice as the date of dissolution, or, if no date of dissolution is mentioned, as from the date of communication of the notice.

22. The Partnership is dissolved on the death or insolvency of any of the Partners or on any of the Partners becoming a mental incompetent so found by a court of law.

23. On dissolution of the Partnership, subject to any contrary agreement binding the former Partners and their estates and after making any necessary adjustments in accordance with generally accepted accounting principles to allow for any debt balances in the Partners' separate capital accounts, the Partnership business shall be promptly liquidated and applied in the following order:

a) to pay the debts and liabilities of the Partnership;
b) to refund any outstanding additional advances, together with accrued interest;
c) to distribution of the credit balances of the Partners' separate income accounts;
d) to distribution of the credit balances of the Partners' capital accounts;
e) to distribution of any residue to the Partners in proportion to their respective Partnership Shares.

ARBITRATION OF DISPUTES

24. Any dispute between the Partners arising out of or related to this agreement and any amendments to it, whether before or after dissolution of the Partnership, shall be referred to and settled by a single arbitrator agreed upon by the Partners, or in default of such agreement, to a single arbitrator appointed pursuant to the legislation governing submissions to arbitration in the jurisdiction whose laws govern this agreement. The decision of the arbitrator is final and binding on the Partners with no right of appeal.

MISCELLANEOUS

25. In this agreement, the singular includes the plural and vice versa unless the context otherwise requires.

26. The capitalized headings in this agreement are only for convenience of reference and do not form part of or affect the interpretation of the agreement.

27. If any provision or part of any provision of this agreement is void for any reason, it shall be severed without affecting the validity of the balance of the agreement.

28. Time is of the essence of this agreement.

29. The terms of this agreement may only be amended in writing dated and signed by all the Partners.

30. This agreement binds and benefits the Partners and their respective heirs, executors, administrators, personal representatives, successors, and assigns.

31. This agreement is governed by the laws of_____

Executed under seal on the _____ day of _____, 20--.

Signed:

_____

Partner   Signature

_____

Partner   Signature

_____

Partner   Signature

Source: Sanderson, Steve, editor, Standard Legal Forms and Agreements, Self- Counsel, Vancouver, Canada, 1989.

General partnerships are quite common among lawyers, doctors, business and management consultants, and small retail store owners.

Advantages of the General Partnership

The following are the major advantages of a general partnership.

1. The general partnership has the ability to raise more capital than the single proprietorship can.
2. The general partnership, like the single proprietorship, is not subject to tax. Individual partners, of course, pay taxes on their incomes, but the partnership business itself pays no tax on its earnings.
3. Discussion is likely to take place among the partners before any important action is taken. These discussions can lead to more sober decisions than those reached by single proprietors who do not need to engage in such discussions. According to the old adage, two heads are better than one.
4. The partnership can benefit from any special talents and skills that the partners possess. One partner may have expertise in marketing, another in management, another in accounting, and so on, and all contribute to the successful operation of the business.
5. Like the single proprietorship, the partnership operates with a minimum of legal restrictions.

Disadvantages of a General Partnership

The general partnership suffers from the following disadvantages.

1. It lacks continuity. If one partner dies or if agreement cannot be reached among the partners, the partnership may have to be dissolved.

2. Although the general partnership may be able to raise more capital than the single proprietor, it is still severely limited in the amount of funds it can raise.

3. The general partnership does have limited liability. This is perhaps its most serious drawback. Each partner in a general partnership is fully liable to the extent of his or her personal possessions for any debts incurred by the business. It is possible for one partner to make a bad business decision in the name of the partnership, thus jeopardizing the financial security of the other partners, because they are severally and jointly liable.

Table 2.2 Summary of the Advantages and Disadvantages of General Partnership

Advantages	Disadvantages
• Increased ability to raise funds	• Lack of continuity
• Possible tax advantage	• Limited ability to raise funds
• Better decisions through discussion	• Unlimited liability
• Minimum legal restrictions	
• Increased talents and skills	

The Limited Partnership

A modified version of the general partnership, called the limited partnership, has emerged. The limited partnership reduces, to a certain extent, the problems of unlimited liability associated with the general partnership. In a limited partnership, certain partners have limited liability. Partners with limited liability are called limited partners. Such partners are liable only to the extent of the amount of money they have invested in the partnership, but they can neither legally take part in managing the business nor conduct any business in the name of the partnership.

A limited partnership requires at least one partner to assume unlimited liability. The limited partnership arrangement increases the ability of the partnership to raise funds because some partners can have limited liability. Knowing that they can lose, at worst, only their investment in the business, limited partners may be attracted to the partnership.

BUSINESS CASE 2.1

Marty Mack and Nancy Nathaniel agree to form a partnership to offer management consulting services to small businesses. Marty and Nancy both have business degrees. They have spent a great deal of time discussing the role that each partner should play, but serious misunderstandings have often occurred. They are constantly debating what was actually said in their discussions.

How might Marty and Nancy resolve this issue?

Answer

It appears that Marty and Nancy have not bothered to draw up a written partnership agreement. Writing up such an agreement will resolve at least some of the misunderstandings.

The Corporation

Let us introduce the concept of a corporation with an illustrative example. We will return to your coffee shop and your college buddy. Your partnership has grown significantly and more and more patrons are visiting the shop. Your current location is now too small, so you and your partner have decided to add another location and increase your product offering, but you need to raise more money for the expansion. Because of the success of your partnership business, other people are willing to invest in your business, but they are reluctant to risk their personal assets. You can overcome this problem by forming a corporation, a business in which all owners have limited liability; they are liable only to the extent of their investment in the business. The corporation exists apart from its owners.

Special Features of the Corporation

The corporation has some interesting features. To begin with, a corporation comes into existence through some act governing the corporation. Those desiring to incorporate, that is, to form a corporation, must apply for and obtain permission from the relevant authorities.

The corporation can raise vast amounts of money by selling shares to those who want to invest in the business. The purchasers of these shares (the shareholders, or stockholders as they are often called) are the owners of the business. A board of directors is elected by the shareholders, and this board hires senior executive officers. The corporation is a legal entity that exists apart from the shareholders. It can sue or be sued, enter into contracts in its own right, and be taxed just like an individual. Not surprisingly, the corporation is the dominant form of business organization in large businesses.

A corporation can be identified by the suffix after its name. The suffix may be something like Ltd (Limited), LLC (Limited Liability Company), Corporation, or Inc. (Incorporated).

Note that in the modern corporation, the decision-making process is often divorced from the risk-taking role, because the risk is borne by the shareholders, who are the owners of the business. A hired manager may not even own shares in the company. The profits of the corporation accrue to the shareholders as dividends. Portions of the profits can be retained to be reinvested in the business. The profits that are not distributed to shareholders are called retained earnings or undistributed profits.

Advantages of the Corporation

The corporation enjoys a number of important advantages, the most important of which are discussed below.

1. It has a tremendous ability to raise huge amounts of money. The shares or stocks of the corporation can easily be transferred from one owner to another. If you hold shares in a corporation, you can sell your shares to any person who is willing to buy them. Investment in corporate stock is thus considered to be very attractive.

2. This form of business organization has the continuity that is lacking in the single proprietorship and the partnership. If a shareholder dies, the corporation continues as usual.

3. The corporation can usually afford to hire the services of experts in different fields. It can hire a staff of researchers, economists, top management personnel, accountants, lawyers, and experts in other fields. Policy decisions are therefore likely to be sound.

4. In a corporation, each owner (shareholder) has **limited liability**, a provision that makes investors in a corporation liable only up to the amount of money they invested in the business. This is undoubtedly the greatest advantage of the corporation.

Disadvantages of the Corporation

Despite the significant advantages of the corporation, it still suffers from the following disadvantages.

1. The earnings of the corporation are taxed twice. The corporation pays a tax on its profits before they are distributed to shareholders as dividends, and the shareholders also pay a tax on their dividends.

2. The owners of the corporation may have little or no control over its operation and those who make the day-to-day decisions

of the corporation may not have the same incentives and objectives as the owners.

3. The size of the corporation often forces a wedge between labour and management. It can also destroy the close personal relationship between owner and customer that is typical of the single proprietorship.

4. It is relatively costly to establish a corporation. In addition to the incorporation fees, the owners may have to hire a lawyer or consultant to draw up the articles of incorporation.

5. The corporation has to comply with numerous government regulations and restrictions, many of which involve some costs to the corporation.

Table 2.3 Summary of the Advantages and Disadvantages of the Corporation

Advantages	Disadvantages
• Tremendous ability to raise large sums of money	• Double taxation
• Continuity	• Separation of ownership and management
• Benefit of professionals	• Labour-management relations may be severed
• Limited liability	• Relatively difficult and costly to establish
	• Subject to many regulations and restrictions

The Cooperative

A cooperative is a business owned, financed, and controlled by its members, who share in the profits and risks in proportion to their patronage. A cooperative is established to reap the benefits of large-scale selling and buying. It is similar to a corporation in many respects.

In fact, it is a modified version of the corporation. A cooperation raises funds by selling shares, and its shareholders enjoy the advantage of limited liability.

Unlike the corporation though, in which a shareholder is entitled to one vote for each share that he or she owns, each member of the cooperative has only one vote no matter how many shares he or she controls. Also, dividends are distributed not in proportion to the number of shares held, as in the case of a corporation, but in proportion to the amount of business that each member conducts with the cooperative.

Different Types of Cooperatives

There are different types of cooperatives and they can be classified according to their main objectives. Thus there are consumer cooperatives, producer cooperatives, purchasing cooperatives, and marketing cooperatives.

Consumer Cooperatives A consumer cooperative is a cooperative formed by consumers to promote their interests. They join together to operate a business that provides consumer goods and services. Because dividends are distributed among the members in proportion to the volume of business each member does with the cooperative (i.e., according to patronage), the members find it advantageous to do as much business as possible with the cooperative.

Producer Cooperatives A producer cooperative is a cooperative formed by producers to protect their interests. The producers believe that by banding together they can better serve their interests. A group of dairy farmers or fruit growers, for example, can form a cooperative for the purpose of increasing efficiency through joint action.

Purchasing and Marketing Cooperatives A purchasing cooperative is a cooperative whose objective is to take advantage of large-scale purchasing. A marketing cooperative is a cooperative whose objective is to take advantage of large-volume selling. By buying on a large scale, a purchasing cooperative can obtain the benefits of lower costs. Similarly, by selling on a large scale, a marketing cooperative can increase its profits.

Advantages of the Cooperative

The cooperative has two main advantages.

1. It can take advantage of the benefits of a large-scale operation. In other words, it can take advantage of economies of scale. For example, a consumer cooperative can obtain supplies more cheaply by buying in large quantities and thus take advantage of quantity discounts. A producer cooperative can establish and operate a distribution system for its products more cheaply than if each producer did his or her own marketing.
2. The managers and customers of a cooperative are likely to work together toward the success of the business. In many cases the managers are also owners.

Disadvantages of the Cooperative

The following are the main disadvantages of the cooperative:

1. It may fail to look beyond its own membership for expert management.
2. The cooperative may be limited by its inability to raise huge amounts of money for two reasons. First, only those individuals who intend conduct a large volume of business with the cooperative are likely to purchase its shares. Second, its members are unlikely to contribute additional funds because dividends are distributed not in proportion to funds invested but rather by patronage.
3. The democratic control that is a feature of cooperatives can limit the quality of decision making severely. The membership

may not be sufficiently informed to vote intelligently on certain major public issues.

Table 2.4 The Advantages and Disadvantages of the Cooperative

Advantages	Disadvantages
• Lower cost of large-scale operation	• May lack expert management
• Cooperation for business success	• Limited ability to raise capital
	• May lack knowledge for effective decision making

Selecting a Form of Business Organization

You now know the major forms of business organization along with their advantages and disadvantages. You are in a position to choose a form that is ideal for your business. Whereas a single proprietorship may be appropriate for a small coffee shop, it may not at all be suitable for a national chain of restaurants. Among the factors to consider in choosing a form of business organization are:

1. The amount of paperwork, legal and otherwise, involved
2. The extent to which you will be liable for the debts of the business
3. The amount of capital that will be required
4. The taxes for which you will be liable
5. The importance of business continuity
6. The cost of establishing the business.

As time progresses, the business may morph into something quite different from its original form, and it may be necessary to change its form of business organization.

CHAPTER 3

BUSINESS FINANCING AND FINANCIAL STATEMENTS

This Photo by Unknown Author is licensed under CC BY-SA

Entrepreneurs need financial statements to keep them informed of their business operations. To operate without them is like driving a vehicle in the dark without lights.

Introduction

You have decided on the form of business organization that is right for your business. Perhaps an even more important decision is how you are going to finance the business. In part, the answer depends on the form of business organization chosen. In this chapter, we consider how the various forms of business organization are financed. We also introduce three main financial statements: the balance sheet, the income statement, and cash flow statement.

Financing a Single Proprietorship

A single proprietorship is financed by the resources of its owner. The owner can raise the capital by borrowing from a financial institution such as a bank or credit union, or from family members and friends. In any case, the financial burden rests squarely on the owner's shoulders.

Financing a Partnership

A partnership is financed similarly to a single proprietorship, except that the financial burden is shared among all of the partners on the basis of some formula that is agreed upon by the partners. Once the business becomes a going concern and begins to earn profits, funds for expansion and new investment can be taken from those profits.

Financing a Corporation

Unlike the single proprietorship and the partnership, the corporation has a number of options that it can use to raise capital. These options can be grouped into two categories: internal and external.

The corporation may decide not to distribute all profits after taxes to its shareholders and to retain a certain amount for reinvestment in the business. Retained earnings provide the main source of funds for investment by businesses.

External financing comes from three main sources: bond issue, bank credit, and shares. Let us examine each of these methods of financing.

Bond Issue A corporation can raise capital by issuing bonds. A bond is interest-bearing evidence of debt issued by a government or corporation. It is a certificate printed on fancy paper that promises to pay a certain amount of money as an interest payment periodically (annually or semi-annually, for example) until the bond matures. The issuer of the bond (the borrower) promises to pay whoever owns it (the lender) the full amount of its face value when the bond becomes due, that is, when it matures.

If you buy a $1,000 bond from a corporation that promises to pay $100 every year for five years, the corporation is actually borrowing $1,000 from you. You will earn $100 every year for five years, and you will receive the principal of $1,000 at the end of the five-year period on the bond's maturity date.

Bank Credit A corporation can negotiate a loan with a bank or other financial institution. The corporation and the lending institution negotiate the terms of the loan. Whereas a bond is usually for a long period, bank credit is usually short-term—up to three years and frequently maturing within a year. The rate of interest that the corporation pays depends largely on the lending institution's evaluation of the degree of risk associated with the corporation. The rate of interest that banks charge their most credit-worthy customers is called the **prime rate**.

Shares A corporation can issue shares. When you buy shares in a company, you are actually buying part of the corporation. As a part owner, you are entitled to a share of the profits, but you must also suffer any losses that may occur.

BUSINESS CASE 3.1

Mr. K. Benjamin has operated a small shipping company for the past 10 years as a single proprietorship. The business has been extremely profitable and the projection for the next five years is fantastic. Mr. Benjamin wants to expand his business and be able to satisfy the fast-growing demand for his services, but this expansion requires a huge injection of capital.

How might Mr. Benjamin deal with this new business situation?

Answer

This seems to be a financing issue. Without limited liability, Mr. Benjamin might find it difficult to raise the necessary capital. He might consider incorporating his company. This will enable him to raise capital by selling shares in his shipping company without exposing his personal assets to risk.

Debt Capital versus Equity Capital

Debt capital is capital raised through bonds and by using credit. It does not entitle you to ownership rights in the company. Equity capital is capital raised from issuing shares and does confer ownership rights in the corporation.

Financial Statements

The financial statements of a business enterprise are records that show its financial results and financial position. There are different types of financial statements, and they are all important because they provide information on different aspects of a business. Among other things, financial statements enable you to know how much debt you owe, the value of your assets, the profits your business is making, your cash-flow situation, etc. In this chapter, we focus on three types of financial statements: the balance sheet, the income statement, and the cash flow statement.

The Balance Sheet

A balance sheet is a financial statement that shows an entity's assets (what it owns), its liabilities (what it owes), and the owners' equity or net worth at a specific time. You will find the following equation to be quite useful:

$$A - L = OE$$

where A = assets, L = liabilities, and OE = owners' equity.

Clearly, the balance sheet is of supreme value to a business enterprise. If the value of its assets is less than the value of its liabilities, then the enterprise faces bankruptcy. That's certainly not a good position for a business to find itself in. Lenders look at the balance sheets of enterprises to help determine whether they will extend loans or credit to them. By periodically studying their balance sheets, business managers can see the direction in which their businesses are going and thus take corrective actions. Table 3.1 illustrates a simple balance sheet for a hypothetical business enterprise.

Table 3.1. Balance Sheet for a Small Business, December 31, 202--

Assets	Amount
Cash	$6,000.00
Inventory	$80,000.00
Prepaid Insurance	$5,000.00
Furniture & Fixtures	$36,000.00
Total Assets	**$127,000.00**
Liabilities & Owner's Equity	
Current Liabilities	$2,000.00

38

Assets	Amount
Loans & Long-term Liabilities	$100,000.00
Owner's Equity	$25,000.00
Total Liabilities & Owner's	**$127,000.00**

The Income Statement

An income statement is a financial statement that shows an entity's revenues, expenses, and profits for a certain period of time such as a year. An income statement is also referred to as a **profit & loss (P & L) statement**. An income statement is important because it enables the managers or owners of the business to quickly determine whether or not the business is profitable. Along with the balance sheet, the income statement is often used by lenders to determine the credit-worthiness of the entity.

The following relations will help you to understand the income statement.

GROSS PROFIT = REVENUE – COST OF GOODS SOLD

OPERATING INCOME = GROSS PROFIT – TOTAL OPERATING EXPENSE

The following table illustrates the income statement of a hypothetical business enterprise.

Table 3.2 Income Statement for a Small Business for the Period January 1 to December 31, 202—

Revenue	$100,000.00
Cost of goods sold	$75,000.00
Gross profit	**$25,000.00**
Operating expenses	
Advertising	$2,000.00
Commissions	$5,000.00
Office supplies	$3,500.00
Office equipment	$2,500.00
Total operating expenses	**$13,000.00**
Operating income	**$12,000.00**
Non-operating income	
Interest income	$5,000.00
Income from sale of investment	$3,000.00
Interest expense	$(500.00)
Loss from lawsuit	$(1,500.00)
Total non-operating income	**$6,000.00**
Net income	**$18,000.00**

The Cash Flow Statement

A cash flow statement is a financial statement that shows the flow of cash into and out of an entity. A business needs to manage its cash flow properly to prevent it from getting into serious trouble. We often hear of businesses experiencing difficulties because of cash flow problems.

Our focus here is to explain briefly the structure and importance of a cash flow statement. The cash flow statement shows the movement of cash associated with three main activities: operating activities, investing activities, and financing activities.

Operating activities include all activities associated with the current production and sale of goods and services. Examples of relevant cash flows associated with operating activities are receipts from sales and wages and salaries. Cash flows related to investing activities include items such as the sale or purchase of assets and loans. Finally, examples of cash flows related to financing activities include the payment of dividends and the payment of debt.

A cash flow statement can be drawn up from the income statement and the balance sheet. An example of a cash flow statement is illustrated in Table 3.3.

Table 3.3. A Cash Flow Statement for a Hypothetical Business for the Year ended December 31, 202--

Cash Flow from Operations	
Net income	$60,000.00
Depreciation	$20,000.00
Increase in Accounts Payable	$10,000.00
Increase in Accounts Receivable	$(20,000.00)
Increase in Inventory	$(30,000.00)
Net Cash from Operations	**$40,000.00**
Cash from Investing Activities	
Purchase of Equipment	$(5,000.00)
Cash from Financing Activities	
Notes Payable	$7,500.00

Cash Flow for Year Ended December 31, 202--	$42,500.00

BUSINESS CASE 3.2

From a relatively early age, Doreen developed a sort of phobia for numbers. Now age 25 and owner of the popular hairdressing salon, **Doreen's**, she is adamant that the only financial statement her business needs is an income statement.

What mistake might Doreen be making?

Answer

Like many small business owners, Doreen might be thinking that all she needs to know is whether or not her business is making a profit, and the income statement (also called the profit and loss statement) is enough to provide that information. However, operating a business requires more information than revenues, expenses, and profits.

The balance sheet, for example, provides much-needed information about the assets, liabilities, and owner's equity of the business. On the other hand, Doreen might want to know where the cash for her business comes from and where it goes, so that she can manage it better.

CHAPTER 4

BUSINESS PLANNING AND BUSINESS MODELING

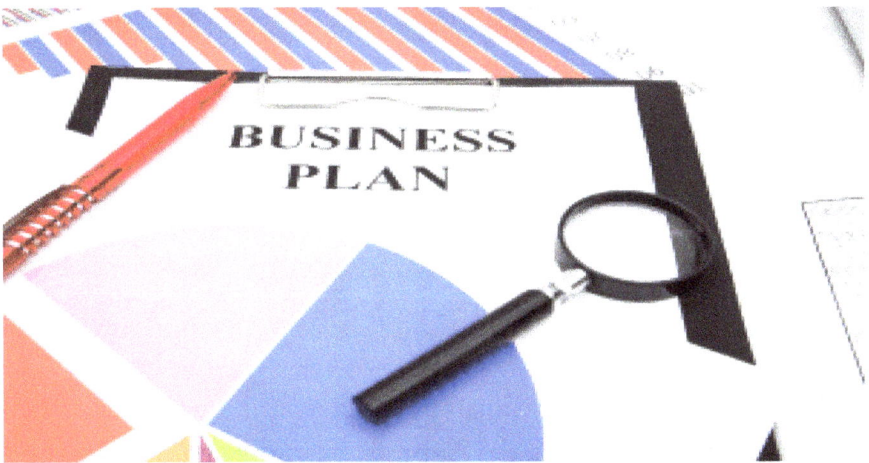

This Photo by Unknown Author is licensed under CC BY-NC-ND

A business without a plan is like a ship without a rudder.

Introduction

You know about the various forms of business organization and which one is appropriate for your business. You also know how each form of business organization is financed, and the importance of financial statements to the successful operation of a business. Before you get too far in the jungle, you must have a clear view of where you want to go and how you are going to get there. That is precisely the purpose of business planning.

A business plan is a fundamental document that outlines in detail an enterprise's objectives and the route it will take to accomplish them. Business planning results in a written road map that guides the firm's marketing, financing, and operational activities. Without such a road map, you are likely to end up hopelessly lost and in the wilderness of bankruptcy.

Many business owners have a business plan drawn up only in response to a request from lenders. This is how the story often goes. You start up a business, and you need to borrow money, so you approach a bank that requires a business plan. You have one drawn up by a consultant or order one from the Internet. You submit your business plan along with the other required documents to the bank, and your loan is approved. You put away your nicely-bound business plan in a drawer in your desk, or in a filing cabinet, never to see daylight again. You attempt to operate your business in the dark (without a plan), and you end up in the wilderness of bankruptcy which is close to the valley of despair.

Always bear in mind that the business plan is your plan and you should have significant input in its development. In this chapter, we discuss the format of a business plan,

The Format of a Business Plan

There is no hard and fast rule for the format of a business plan, but experts generally agree that they should contain the following:

- Executive Summary
- Company Summary
- Products/Services
- Market Analysis Summary

- Strategy and Implementation Summary
- Management Summary
- Financial Plan
- Appendix

Executive Summary

The executive summary is often the last part of the business plan to be written. It contains the objectives of the business, its vision (how you see the business at some future date), its mission (the primary goal of the business), and the major keys to business success.

Business Summary

This section gives an overview of the business. It contains information about the ownership of the company, the form of business organization (that is, single proprietorship, partnership, or corporation), start-up summary outlining cost of equipment, licences, and permits, advertising, start-up inventory, insurance, etc., and business location and facilities.

Product/Service

Here is the place in your business plan where you carefully describe your product/service. Specificity is important here. If you are selling coffee, it is more effective to describe the product as coffee rather than hot drinks. List your closest competitors and state how your product/service differs from those of your competitors. In this section also, you identify your suppliers and how you plan to establish and maintain a relationship with them. State the role that technology will play in assisting you to acquire and sell your product/service. Any new product/service that you plan to add should be included here.

Market Analysis

In this section, you should clearly identify your market. What is its size in terms of potential customers and sales? What segment of the market do you plan to serve? What strategy do you plan to use to reach the chosen segment of the market? Consider any specific needs of this market segment and state how to plan to satisfy these needs. Take note of any trends, including growth and how they will affect your operation. Identify the industry in which you plan to operate and state whether it is highly competitive, monopolistically competitive, monopolistic, or oligopolistic.

SWOT Analysis

SWOT stands for **s**trengths, **w**eaknesses, **o**pportunities, and **t**hreats. In business planning, it is of vital importance for you to know your firm's strengths, weaknesses, opportunities, and threats. SWOT analysis gives you the opportunity to capitalize on your firm's strengths, eliminate or reduce its weaknesses, seize relevant opportunities, and respond appropriately to prevailing or future threats.

Strategy and Implementation

This is a substantive part of your business plan because it points out the actions that you will take to accomplish your goals. It usually follows the SWOT analysis because it relies on information from the SWOT analysis. It typically includes your firm's competitive edge, the value proposition (how your customers will benefit from doing business with you), actions you will take to increase sales (sales strategy), expected future sales, marketing strategy, sales programs, positioning statement (where you plan to situate your business in the market), pricing strategy, how you plan to promote the business. In this section, you will also indicate any strategic alliances you plan to form that will enhance the business.

Management

The success of a business enterprise depends crucially on decisions made by its management. This section of the business plan outlines the organizational structure of the enterprise, the personnel plan, and the management team along with their expertise and experiences. If there are gaps in management, you should point them out and explain how you plan to fill them.

Financial Plan

The fact that the financial plan is usually the last part of the business plan does not diminish its importance in any way. The financial plan is based on key assumptions. You should spell out these assumptions. In this section, you should indicate how much money will be needed, where it will come from, what it will be used for, and how loans, if any, will be repaid. A break-even analysis is often included. The material presented in the previous chapter will prove to be quite useful here. Among the financial statements that you should include are pro forma income statement, balance sheet, and cash flow statement.

Appendix

The final section of the business plan is an appendix. It contains any information that you would like the readers to have, but is not included in any previous section. The appendix may include items such as resumés of the principals of the business; graphs, charts, and tables that support the plan; contracts and agreements relevant to your business; and relevant licenses and permits.

Updating the Business Plan

Recall that the first copy of your business plan was based on the current state of affairs and your *perception* of what the future will be. The uncertainties and unknowns of the future make it absolutely essential to update the plan. That which was once uncharted territory has now become familiar waters. For example, when you drafted your first business plan, you thought that radio ads would be most effective. Now, after six months in business, you know that your website is by far your most effective medium. An updated business plan will reflect such facts.

Events that may Trigger a Plan Update

Events that may trigger an update of your plan include the following:

A lowering of prices by your closest competitors This action by your competitors requires some kind of reaction on your part. Options available to you might be to leave your prices unchanged or to follow suit and lower your prices as well. In any event, it is likely that your revenue will be affected. Will you respond by increasing your advertising budget, by extending your operating hours, or by adopting some other strategy? An update of your business plan will be in order.

Changes in economic conditions Your initial business plan made certain assumptions about economic variables such as unemployment, inflation, and interest rates. Changes in these variables will affect your business plan. For example, an increase in unemployment will make it more difficult for customers to purchase your product/service, inflation will make your supplies more expensive, and higher interest rates will make it more difficult to finance your operation. In such circumstances, your initial business plan will be obsolete.

Changes in taxes Your initial projections were based on the existing tax provisions. The imposition of new taxes or the withdrawal of existing ones will certainly influence some aspect of your business. An increase in the sales tax will negatively affect your sales, a reduction in property taxes will reduce your operating cost, and an increase in profit taxes will reduce your profits before taxes. These changes will necessitate a review of your business plan.

Changes in key management personnel The success of your business depends crucially on decisions made my management. Changes in key management personnel may actually change the direction of the firm and dictate an update of your business plan.

The implementation of new technology As time passes, you upgrade your machines and employ new technology in your business operation. These upgrades affect the number of employees required, the time it takes to complete a given task, the delivery of services to your clients, and other areas of your business. Under such circumstances, you should consider bringing your business plan up to date.

Changes in public policy Public policies often have significant impacts on businesses. For example, subsidies to farmers have positive effects on both producers and consumers of farm products. To keep your business plan relevant, it should be updated when the business is affected by changes in public policy.

BUSINESS CASE 4.1

Bob: Let's make sure we get this business plan right so that we avoid the expense of having to revise it.

Peter: I agree completely with you. This is our roadmap to success, and having to revise it is not a viable option.

What misconception about a business plan is shared by Bob and Peter?

Answer

Bob and Peter seem to be under the misconception that a business plan is a permanent inflexible document. It is true that no effort should be spared in making sure that the business plan is as realistic as possible, but circumstances change, and when they do, it might be necessary to update the business plan to keep it relevant.

Uses of a Business Plan

We indicated earlier that many business plans originate from a request by lenders. A business plan is an essential document for a business enterprise borrowing money from a bank or seeking capital from investors. Although its primary use may be to raise money, a business plan has many other uses, some of which are given in this section.

In the same way as a rudder is used to keep a ship on course, so too a business plan can be used to keep a business on target. Following the establishment of the business, the managers should frequently compare the actual results with the planned outcomes, and appropriate adjustments should be made. This way, the business plan is used as a guide steering the business to the accomplishment of its desired goals.

A business plan dictates the kind of talent that is needed to successfully lead the business. Thus, it is an important help in the recruiting process. If the plan calls for a marketing expert with at least five years of experience in the field, then the recruiting effort will be geared toward that end.

A business plan forces you to become familiar with your product/service and the market you plan to serve. Is your product/service in high demand? Is the demand likely to hold steady, rise, or fall during the next three to five years? How serious is the threat from new competitors? What adjustments will you make to deal with these threats? What strategies will you use to grow your business? For how long will your current location be adequate? A business plan will enable you to answer these and other pertinent questions regarding your business.

Business Modeling

Business modeling is the process of deciding exactly how a business will make money. You must be careful not to confuse a business model with a business plan. Whereas a business plan is a detailed guide outlining the various strategies that you will use to accomplish your business' mission and vision, a business model is a much less elaborate document summarizing exactly how your business will generate revenues and earn profits. Table 3.1 below shows the business model of a hypothetical coffee shop.

Why you need a Business Model

It is safe to state that one of the main reasons for starting a business is to earn a profit. A business may provide you with a job, provide an opportunity for you to do something that you really enjoy, give you significant satisfaction as a business owner, or enhance your status in the community; but it is unlikely that many people will venture into business knowing that they will lose money.

A business model forces you to focus on how your business will earn a profit. For example, you would not normally use a business model that consistently requires you to purchase items at $95.00 each and sell them at a price of $90.00 each, because by so doing, you would lose money.

A business model can form the basis of a business plan. For example, the business model identifies the basic characteristics of the customers you need to attract in order for your business to be profitable. The business plan outlines the tactics and strategies that you will use to attract those customers. As another example, the business model states who will manage the business, while the business plan specifies the qualifications and experiences required of the managers and explains how any gaps in managerial skills will be remedied.

Table 4.1 Business Model for a hypothetical Coffee Shop

Components	Explanation
Company	A-B Coffee Delight (Name is tentative)
Management	The firm will be managed by its founders, Alan Anthony and Bertrand Browne. Professional support will come from suitably qualified consultants.
Employees	Initially, the business will hire one employee to help the owners. As the business expands, additional workers will be employed. All employees will be carefully screened.
Location	At start-up, A-B Coffee Delight will be located at 123 Main Street, Any Town, Any Country.
Major Business Activity	The firm will provide a wide variety of coffee in a relaxing environment. It will also carry a wide variety of pastries. It will offer both "sit down" and "take out" services.
Value proposition	A-B Coffee Delight's products and service will be of the highest quality. The products will be fresh and competitively priced, and patrons will be assured that they will receive value for money.
Customers	Our customers will include coffee lovers, pastry lovers, people who want to relax in a pleasant environment, and people on the run. A major part of our customers will be people who rely on us for breakfast.
Customer relationship	A-B Coffee Delight will develop and maintain strong business relationships with our patrons. We will establish strong and effective communication with them, treating them as partners in the process.

Components	Explanation
Customer channels	A-B Coffee Delight intends to use a variety of channels to communicate with its customers. These channels can include radio, television, the print media, the Internet, and word of mouth.
Activity type	The activity type can be classified as fast food service.
Capital	Currently, A-B Coffee Delight is being financed from the owners' personal resources. Additional equity capital may be sought through a private placement.
Revenue	The sale of coffee and pastries will be the main revenue source for A-B Coffee Delight.
Pricing strategy	The business will examine various pricing models before adopting one. With regard to pricing, we will pay keen attention to the feasibility of the quick sale-light profit maxim where sales volume is critical. In pricing for profit, we will estimate the demand elasticities for our products and price accordingly.
Cost structure	Major operational cost elements will be the cost of our equipment (machines), rent, furniture and fixtures, advertising, and wages. Regular market analyses will also entail significant cost.

BUSINESS CASE 4.2

To the trained eye, it is obvious that a business plan is totally unnecessary if you have a good business model.

Comment on this statement.

Answer

There is a common misconception in some quarters that a business plan and a business model are one and the same thing, and that misconception is being perpetuated in the above statement. Although a business plan and a business are related, they are by no means identical. The business model tells specifically how the business is going to make money. Its focuses precisely on how the business is going to make a profit. A business plan, on the other hand, is a detailed road map pointing out the route that should be taken in order for a business to successfully achieve its mission and vision. The entrepreneur needs both.

CHAPTER 5

PROFITS

Profits can be seen as a reward for entrepreneurial services and as a motivation for the entrepreneur.

Introduction

Most people will agree that entrepreneurs start businesses because of the prospect of profits. Whereas it may be disputed that the main objective of entrepreneurs is to maximize profits, the vast majority of people will likely agree that rational entrepreneurs will not want to operate businesses if they knew that they will earn no profits. In this chapter, we discuss the meaning of profits,

The Meaning of Profits

Let's be clear about what we mean by profits. **Profits** refer to the difference between the revenues obtained from the sale of goods and services and the expenses incurred in producing the goods and services. This difference is also referred to as **net income**. The profit for Winston's Cabinet Shop (hypothetical) is shown as:

Total revenue	$50,000
Total expenses	$40,000
Profit ($50,000 - $40,000)	$10,000

The entrepreneur has to decide if this profit is sufficient to keep him in this business.

Other Perspectives from which to view Profits

There are other ways of looking at profits. Profits can be viewed as a return on innovation, as a reward for taking risks, or as the result of market power. It's a good idea to examine profits from each of these different perspectives.

Profit as a Return on Innovation and Entrepreneurial Ability Why do people decide to own their own business enterprises rather than sell their factor services to others? One reason is the prospect of greater profits. Presumably, many people feel that they have better insight, more imagination, and are more adventurous than anyone they have worked for or can work for. If these people are indeed as innovative as they think and their innovations succeed, then they are compensated with profits. If they fail, they suffer losses.

Profit as a Reward for Risk-taking No matter how shewed entrepreneurs may be, they must confront the risks involved in owning their own businesses. Profits are sometimes viewed as a reward for bearing the risks of business ownership—a sort of risk premium. In the absence of this risk premium, many people would not consider it worthwhile to bear the risks associated with business ownership.

Profit from Market Power A firm with significant market power, such as a monopoly, may be able to earn profits simply because of its ability to exercise some control price. Such firms may benefit from effective barriers to entry such as patent rights, and control of essential resources.

Business Role of Profits

Profits perform some important business functions:

1. They serve as a signal to entrepreneurs.
2. They provide a motive for incentive for efficiency in business operations
3. They reward the resourceful or enterprising.

Profit as a Signal to Entrepreneurs The existence of profits in any industry or sector of the economy is a clear signal that price exceeds the average cost of production and that entrepreneurs will do well to shift resources into that industry or sector of the economy. Likewise, the existence of losses in an industry is a loud and clear signal to entrepreneurs that resources should be shifted out of the industry and put to more productive and profitable uses.

Profit as a Motive for Efficiency The desire for profits serves as an incentive for entrepreneurs to cut production costs where possible. In the face of competition, high-cost firms will lose their market shares to low-cost firms. Unless high-cost firms can increase their efficiency, they will ultimately be forced out of the market.

Profit as a Reward Profits serve as a reward for the resourceful, the imaginative, the innovative, and the enterprising. The prospect of earning profits is often the driving force behind the development and maintenance of special resources and talents.

BUSINESS CASE 5.1

Justin is a business student at Best Business College. After studying the sources of various forms of income, he concluded that there is no rational business justification for profit-taking.

To what extent is Justin correct?

Answer

Justin's conclusion is totally false. Resources are the only source of income. Those resources can be classified as natural resources, human resources, capital, and entrepreneurial services. The income derived from natural resources is rent, the income derived from human resources is called wages and salaries, the income derived from capital is interest and dividends, and the income derived from entrepreneurial services is profit.

Any objection to profit-taking as rational is a denial of the services provided by entrepreneurs. Entrepreneurs assume the risk of organizing natural resources, human resources, and capital into production. Profit is the income from their services, and it is totally justifiable.

Requirements for Profit Success

Profit is not something that just happens in a vacuum. If you know the requirements for long-term profit success, you can more effectively pursue your goal of earning profits. Here, we identify three requirements for long-term profit success:

- Serve growth markets
- Develop and maintain a competitive edge
- Aim for profit stability

Serve Growth Markets

Entrepreneurs that expect to earn profits in the future must find a way to serve growth markets successfully. If your market is dwindling, it will most likely be reflected in your profit margin. Successful entrepreneurs must actively pursue opportunities to serve markets that are growing and have the potential to grow.

Develop and Maintain a Competitive Edge

Consistently high-profit margins and high returns on investment are supported by one or more of several forms of competitive advantage. Entrepreneurs must be aware of three key functional abilities that can provide a competitive advantage to capitalize on market and other changes.

- Marketing strength in a small business services delivery system and related marketing practices
- Product/service development—development or acquisition of new products or services.
- Productivity—increasing pressure for lower costs through greater productivity.

Aim for Profit Stability

Although it may be difficult to achieve profit stability in a small business environment with a single product/service or a single-market operation, it is entirely possible. Some entrepreneurs have actually formulated three or five year plans for profits. Profits are more likely to be stable within a planning environment.

Steps in Profit Planning

Profits should not be left to chance. Entrepreneurs should realize that they can plan for profit. By planning for profit, they avoid viewing profit from operations as nothing but a residual over which they have little or no control. We will show how entrepreneurs can plan their business operations in such a way that they earn the profits that can reasonably be expected.

Analysis of Business Activities

The first step in planning for profits is the analysis of the business' record of operations to date with respect to profitability, growth, and other measures versus those of competitors and the total industry to which the business belongs. Measures of performance may include:

- Return on investment
- Growth of earnings
- Sales
- Profits
- Equity
- Cash flow

Setting Standards

Establishing standards for future accomplishment is the second step in profit planning. These standards will vary by type of business. A particular business may face the problem of maintaining an attractive profit record. This could very well be its standard for the future. Another firm's standard may be to raise its return to the average of the industry.

In many instances, the industry average will be the important factor in setting goals or standards; but even this can be elusive. A particular entrepreneur could have difficulty determining the *industry average* because the operating ratios of the various firms in the industry vary too widely to give meaning to an average. This wide variation is attributable to the fact that included in a particular industry are several different types of firms. In agriculture, for example, there are different kinds of farms, such as those specializing in vegetables, those specializing in rice, those specializing in milk production, those specializing in chicken, those specializing in beef, and those offering a wide range of agricultural products.

Projections

The third step in the profit planning process is a five-year or possibly a ten-year projection of sales and profits and the resultant investment at expanded levels of present operations. This is a normal outcome of effective market analysis. In making these projections, entrepreneurs should do so in the light of the opportunities and threats facing present businesses. The longer the projection period, other things being equal, the greater the number of revisions that will be necessary to keep projections up to date.

Extent of the Need for New Products or Services

The measurement of the extent of the need for new products (the difference between the standards of future profits and the projections of present products) is the fourth step in profit planning. A combination of this and the previous step provides a schedule of long-term objectives of sales, profits, and capital requirements for present and future (new) products or services. It goes without saying that the financial resources of an entrepreneur may determine the feasibility of the objectives.

The Profit Plan

At this stage, the entrepreneur reviews the proposed profit plan and makes any necessary changes. Changes normally reflect inconsistencies in strategic objectives or in timing of events. After the review and adjustments are completed, the entrepreneur adopts a formal profit plan that reflects objectives and overall action plans.

Plan Implementation

The final phase of profit planning is the establishment of a timetable for implementing the plan. This requires the assignment of responsibilities and accurate data so that planned results can be compared with actual results.

BUSINESS CASE 5.2

Charles and Veron are both young entrepreneurs who hold opposing views on profits. Charles views profits as the result of hard work and luck. He considers profit-planning a big waste of time that does not work. Veron, on the other hand, is a strong advocate of profit planning. She believes that although entrepreneurs cannot totally control their profits, they can influence them to some extent.

Who is right?

Answer

In this case, Veron is correct. Through profit planning, entrepreneurs can establish a number of strategies to be taken in order to accomplish a targeted amount of profit. This way, the achievement of profits is not merely luck and hard work.

CHAPTER 6

BUDGETING

This Photo by Unknown Author is licensed under CC BY-NC

A budget is an important tool for helping entrepreneurs achieve their revenue and expenditure goals.

Introduction

Briefly stated, a budget is an estimate of expected revenues and expenditures for a given period of time. Budgeting, in general, is the process of determining target revenues and expenses by component and by department if applicable. In the same way that it is prudent for a household to live within its budget, so too it is crucially important for entrepreneurs to draw up budgets for their businesses and be guided by those budgets in order to avoid financial ruin.

This chapter contains information on budget positions, types of budgets, and budget monitoring. The chapter also lists a number of common budgeting problems that you should avoid.

Budget Positions

Budget deficit, budget surplus, and balanced budget are terms often used in discussions of spending and revenues. At any given time, the budget can be in only one of the following positions: a budget deficit, a budget surplus, or a balanced budget. Let us define each of these terms.

Budget Deficit

A budget deficit is a condition that exists when spending is greater than revenues. The size of the deficit is the difference between spending (S) and revenues (R):

$$\text{Budget deficit} = S - R$$

For example, if in 2022 the firm's total revenues amounted to $650,000 and its total spending was $700,000, then it had a budget deficit of ($700,000 – 650,000) = $50,000 in 2022.

Budget Surplus

A **budget surplus** is a condition that exists when spending by an entity is less than its revenues during a period of time. The size of the surplus is the difference between revenues (R) and spending (S):

$$\text{Budget surplus} = R - S$$

For example, if in 2021 the firm's total revenues amounted to $580,000 and its total spending was $570,000, then it had a budget surplus of $10,000 in 2021.

Balanced Budget

A **balanced budget** is the situation that exists when an entity currently spends exactly as much as it earns in revenues during a period of time. The entity is just breaking even.

$$\text{Balanced budget: } S = R$$

For example, a business enterprise would have a balanced budget if it collected $600,000 in revenues in a given year and spent $600,000 in the same year.

The Importance of a Budget

The importance of budgeting for business operations can hardly be exaggerated. Budgeting has the following advantages:

Minimizes Unplanned Spending

The budgeting process helps entrepreneurs estimate business revenue, enables them to carefully plan their expenses, and encourages them to avoid any spending not called for in the budget. Thus, resources are allocated to their planned purposes.

Improves Communication

Communication is an important ingredient in business success. Budgeting is an effective means of communicating targeted goals and the means of achieving them.

Monitors Performance

Budgeting enables entrepreneurs to monitor the performance of their businesses. If actual revenues and expenditures vary appreciably from the budgeted figures, then the variances can be analyzed and corrective actions can be taken to bring operations back on track.

Motivates Employees

It is an undeniable fact that success is a tremendous motivator. If you are achieving the desired results from an activity, you will be driven to expend even greater effort on that activity. Budgeting helps businesses achieve their profit objectives. They are thus able to pay better wages and other benefits to their employees, and this motivates them.

Avoids Financial Dilemmas

If you don't keep track of revenues and expenses, you are likely to find yourself in a situation where your expenses exceed your revenues, and if this situation continues unnoticed or ignored, bankruptcy can result. Careful budgeting can avert this eventuality.

Budget Types

A business can prepare many different types of budgets including, capital budget, cash budget, financial budget, labour budget, marketing budget, operating budget, production budget, and sales budget. The types of budgets that will be relevant depend on the nature of the business enterprise. Although all budgets have their purposes, we will limit our discussion to two types of budgets: cash budget and operating budget.

Cash Budget

Regardless of the nature of the business, it is most likely that it will need cash to carry on its normal operation. Cash flow problems have been the bane of many entrepreneurs. In the absence of a cash budget, the business could find itself with too much idle cash on hand, or not enough cash to enable it to meet its normal financial obligations. The cash budget shows the timing of cash receipts and disbursements.

The first step in drawing up a cash budget is to prepare an estimate of cash receipts for any given period. Service sales and cash receipts forecast, along with the firm's normal collection period (if applicable) will provide an estimate of cash receipts. Entrepreneurs must then consider the uses of cash. This information may be obtained from expenditure plans.

The following is an example of a cash budget for a hypothetical small business enterprise for a two-month period.

Table 6.1 Hypothetical Cash Budget

Item	May	June
Cash at beginning of month	$1,000	$1,500
Receipts	5,000	5,400
Total	6,000	6,900
Cash disbursements	4,500	5,000
Cash at end of month	1,500	1,900

If entrepreneurs were in a position where their cash disbursements exceeded their cash receipts, they would probably have to arrange for additional cash. The amount of additional cash would then be shown as an item in the cash budget and would have been added to total cash. Any cash outflow resulting from the arrangement should be shown as an item in the cash budget and would have been added to total cash disbursements.

Operating Budget

An operating budget shows all revenues and expenses that the business plans to have as a result of its operations. An example of an operating budget is presented below.

Table 6.2 Hypothetical Operating Budget

Item	Budgeted Amount
Revenue:	
Gross revenue	$20,000,000
Cost of stock (goods)	6,000,000
Net revenue	14,000,000
Revenues from services	700,000
Gross profit	$14,700,000
Expenses:	
Salaries	$1,000,000
Theft and bad debts	8,000,000
Rent	100,000
Telephone	100,000
Travelling	60,000
Training	10,000
Office supplies	70,000
Heat, electricity and water	150,000
Entertainment	50,000
Bank charges & interest	800,000
Building maintenance	60,000
Insurance	150,000
Automobile expenses	40,000
Group expenses	150,000
Directors' fees	200,000
Repairs & maintenance	80,000
Advertising & promotion	200,000
Miscellaneous	20,000
Total	11,240,000
Profit before income tax	**3,460,000**

Budget Monitoring

The main purpose of a budget is to keep the entrepreneur on track. If budgeted results are simply ignored, then the time, energy, effort, and money spent on creating budgets will be sadly lost. Budget monitoring is the process of comparing the actual results with the budgeted figures and then taking steps to address the variance. Table 6.3 shows the budget monitoring process.

Table 6.3 Budget Monitoring Process

Item	Budgeted	Actual	Variance
Revenue:			
Gross revenue	$20,000,000	$21,500,000	+$1,500,000
Cost of stock (goods)	6,000,000	4,500,00	-1,500,000
Net revenue	14,000,000	17,000,000	+3,000,000
Revenues from services	700,000	600,000	-100,000
Gross profit	$14,700,000	$17,600,000	+$2,900,000
Expenses:	$1,000,000	$1,500,000	+$500,000
Salaries			
Theft and bad debts	8,000,000	8,050,000	+$50,000
Rent	100,000	100,000	Nil
Telephone	100,000	110,000	+$10,000
Travelling	60,000	100,000	+$40,000
Training	10,000	10,000	Nil
Office supplies	70,000	65,000	-$5,000
Heat, electricity and water	150,000	140,000	-$10,000
Entertainment	50,000	49,000	-$1,000
Bank charges & interest	800,000	799,000	-$1,000

Item	Budgeted	Actual	Variance
Building maintenance	60,000	60,000	Nil
Insurance	150,000	150,000	Nil
Automobile expenses	40,000	40,000	Nil
Group expenses	150,000	150,000	Nil
Directors' fees	200,000	200,000	Nil
Repairs & maintenance	80,000	78,000	-$2,000
Advertising & promotion	200,000	200,000	Nil
Miscellaneous	20,000	25,000	+$5,000
Total	**11,240,000**	**11,826,000**	**+$586,000**
Profit before income tax	**3,460,000**	**5,774,000**	**+$2,324,000**

In this example, the actual gross revenue figure exceeded the planned or budgeted figure by $1,500,000, and the actual cost of goods was less than the budgeted by $1,500,000. This led to net revenue of $3,000,000 over the budgeted figure of $14,000,000. Actual revenues from services were $100,000 less than the budgeted amount. The result of all this was gross profits of $2,900,000 over the budgeted amount.

Labor cost turned out to be $500,000 more than the budgeted amount. A variance of this magnitude deserves some attention. Was it unavoidable? Did this business hire more employees than were necessary? Was the budgeted figure unrealistic to begin with? These are questions that must be answered, and appropriate measures must be taken. Notice that the rent, advertising, and insurance figures came in right on target. This could be due to contractual agreements for these items. Variances in the other items were relatively small, except for travelling and theft and bad debts. Entrepreneurs need to take a good look at large variances with a view to instituting corrective measures.

Budget monitoring should be a regular feature in running a business so that significant variances can be detected and analyzed and appropriate actions taken to safeguard the profitability of the business.

BUSINESS CASE 6.1

Pete has just completed a comparison of his operating budget figures with the actual figures and found that over 87% of the figures were right on target. Delighted with the performance of his business, Pete suggested to his wife, Mary, that in their next budget, they should change only the few items that were off target.

Is this good budget planning on Pete's part?

Answer

This is awful budget planning. Pete seems to be assuming that business is static. Nothing can be further from the truth. Business conditions are constantly changing. What worked last month may not work this month. A good entrepreneur must be ready to embrace and react appropriately to change. Adjusting only those items that were off target is a recipe for disaster. Pete would do well to reconsider his stance.

Common Budgeting Problems to Avoid

There are many problems that may be encountered in the budgeting process. In this section, we point out some of them so that you, the entrepreneur, will be prepared and take care to avoid them.

Lack of Discipline

Budgeting requires discipline. It is painstaking work but it must be done in order to ensure success. Without a certain measure of self-discipline, entrepreneurs will tend to put a few schedules together and refer to them as budgets. This tendency must be resisted. As an entrepreneur, you must be prepared to spend the necessary time in collecting and estimating budget data. In budgeting, discipline is a virtue.

Failure to learn from Experience

Budgeting is based on estimates, but the estimates must be based on knowledge and judgment, not wishful thinking. The performance of previous budgets is a good source of knowledge for future budget preparation. Review your previous years' budgets to identify areas where you had expense overruns and revenue shortfalls. Identify the reasons and implement action plans to eliminate these occurrences. This will help in enabling you to come up with more accurate data for your next year's budget.

Failure to Consider Shorter Periods

A budget is a control device. If entrepreneurs prepare a budget for an entire year, as they often do, and then compare the budgeted figures with the actual figures a year later, they could encounter serious problems. Failure to select an appropriate period for budget review is a common problem in budgeting. If entrepreneurs prepare a budget for a year, they should, if practical, break down the one-year period into smaller periods such as a quarter or even a month. This will allow tighter control over business operations.

Omission of an Allowance for Unexpected Expenses

It is the nature of business to experience periods of unexpected expenses. Whereas rent, insurance, and wages may be expected, an unforeseen increase in the cost of raw materials, or a sudden increase in the price of fuel is not outside the realm of possibility. The failure to plan for unexpected expenses is a mistake that entrepreneurs should try to avoid. In budgeting, some businesses create an emergency fund to which they allocate about 5% of their budgeted expenses to cover such unexpected expenses. This emergency fund allows them to address unexpected expenses without disrupting the financial stability of the business.

Failure to Analyze Variances

Many entrepreneurs behave as if the budgeting process is complete as soon as they have finalized the preparation of the budget. Little or no budget monitoring occurs. If entrepreneurs analyze the differences between the budgeted figures and the actual performance figures, then they will hardly be able to take corrective measures. The analysis of variance is a crucial aspect of the budgeting process and should not be neglected.

Failure to Set Realistic Goals

In a sense, budgeting is an exercise in goal setting. Optimism may be a good quality for entrepreneurs to possess, but setting unrealistic goals in budgeting is definitely counterproductive. If you overestimate your revenues and underestimate your expenses, your targeted profit will be unrealistic. It makes better business sense to set realistic targets and then find ways to increase revenues and reduce expenses, thus improving the financial health of the business.

Keeping the Budget a Secret

A budget is not your personal secret device for operating your business. Instead, it is a plan of action to help you to achieve certain targeted goals. The entrepreneur depends on other stakeholders to play their roles in the success of the business. Sharing the budget with them gives them a sense of direction as well as guidelines to follow in pursuit of their goals. Keeping the budget a secret is a mistake that should be avoided.

Failure to Act

Another problem with budgeting is failure on the part of entrepreneurs to take necessary actions. Let us assume that after analyzing the labour budget variance, it becomes obvious that the number of employees should be reduced. But some entrepreneurs, for a variety of reasons, find it difficult to take the appropriate action, which, in this case, is laying off some workers. Often, success as an entrepreneur requires the ability to make tough decisions.

BUSINESS CASE 6.2

In a fiercely competitive business environment, an entrepreneur must take measures to ensure that not even the right hand knows what the left hand is doing. Too many businesses have bitten the dust because others have stolen and implemented their plans. That is why it is of utmost importance to keep the budget a safely guarded secret.

Comment on the advice above.

Answer

This kind of advice is not worth heeding. Following it could be detrimental to a business. A budget is designed for a particular business surrounded by a particular set of circumstances, so a budget prepared for business A will unlikely be suitable for budget B. The implementation of a business budget will usually require participation from other stakeholders. Keeping the budget from them is tantamount to asking them to run in the dark. Leaving them out of the equation is not only unwise but impractical.

CHAPTER 7

PRICING DECISIONS

This Photo by Unknown Author is licensed under CC BY

If entrepreneurs don't know how to price their goods and services, they could bankrupt their businesses.

Introduction

The pricing of goods and services is one of the most important business decisions that entrepreneurs have to make. If the goods and services are priced too low, customers may be attracted, but the business may fail to cover its operating cost. Too high a price can result in a loss of market share that might spell disaster for the business.

Simply defined, price is value expressed in terms of money. If item 1 is priced at $10 while item 2 is priced at $20, I get the feeling that item 2 is twice as valuable as item 1. Pricing is the process of allocating prices to items. As an entrepreneur, you want your customers to know the values of the goods and services that you are selling. This information is transmitted by pricing. Topics that will be discussed in this chapter include pricing objectives, pricing strategies, pricing services, changing prices, and changing prices.

Pricing Objectives

Entrepreneurs have different objectives, and pricing is one means by which they can achieve those objectives. Let us take a look at some of the common objectives that may be achieved by pricing.

Customer Retention

Entrepreneurs know that without customers there can be no business. Hence, they spend significant amounts of money on customer acquisition. Once they acquire the customers, they must try to retain them. Pricing can be a means of retaining customers. If you use price as a means of retaining customers, you must bear in mind that price-sensitive customers will tend to leave following a price increase.

Profit Maximization

Whether entrepreneurs seek to maximize profits or to earn a satisfactory profit, pricing can be a means of achieving their ends. One thing is sure: a business that does not earn any profit will not long continue to operate. The objective here is to try to increase revenues and reduce expenses. Price can play a role.

Increasing Sales

The growth of sales is another objective that pricing can be used to achieve. Whether the sales growth results from customers switching from competitors or from new customers entering the market, pricing can influence both. In using prices to increase sales volume, entrepreneurs must be careful not to set prices so low that they incur losses.

Survival Pricing

A business may find itself in survival mode. In such a case, it is hanging on for dear life as the saying goes, and other objectives give way to staying alive. Survival pricing involves setting a price that allows the firm to stay in business while at the same time covering essential costs. Clearly, survival pricing is intended to be used only on a short-term basis.

Create a Perception of Fairness

An entrepreneur may use pricing to create and maintain an image of fairness. If customers perceive that you practice fair pricing, they will tend to believe that you are fair in other aspects of business operations and will develop confidence in doing business with you. Also, the practice of fair pricing may be a means of preventing the authorities from controlling your prices.

BUSINESS CASE 7.1

Business student 1: I do not understand why Mr. Gordon, proprietor of the Corner Store, does not increase his prices. It is obvious that he could earn more profits just by raising his prices. Do you understand why he doesn't raise his prices?

Business student 2: You and I are in the same boat. I am also baffled by Mr. Gordon's decision not to raise his prices. Maybe we should have a talk with him.

What important fact might these business students be overlooking?

Answer

The business students seem to be of the opinion that Mr. Gordon's objective is to maximize his profits. Perhaps they have not reached that point in their studies where the objectives of firms are discussed, or maybe they have just forgotten. The fact is, profit maximization might not be Mr. Gordon's objective. For example, he might be perfectly satisfied with a certain level of profits, or he might be trying to increase sales, or attain some other objective.

Pricing Strategies

Limit Pricing

Limit pricing is the deliberate setting of prices so low that new entrants into the market will make no profits. Limit pricing, also called predatory pricing, is used as a barrier to the entry of new firms into the market.

Cost-Plus Pricing

Cost-plus pricing is a pricing method whereby a firm determines its selling price by adding a certain percentage markup to its cost. For example, if the firm's cost of an item is $12, it may choose a markup of 25% and set its price at $15. This method of pricing helps entrepreneurs to determine their profits. Cost-plus pricing is also known as markup pricing.

Competitive Pricing

Many entrepreneurs adopt this pricing strategy because it is relatively easy to implement. It involves finding out what your competitors are charging and then charging a similar price. Under certain conditions, you may consider setting your price slightly above or below theirs, but not considerably different.

Price Skimming

This idea is analogous to skimming the cream off the top. The entrepreneur starts by setting a high price, thus appealing to those customers who are willing and able to pay that price. Then, as the market evolves, he or she lowers the price.

Penetration Pricing

This pricing strategy is used by new firms trying to penetrate the market. It entails setting a low price initially to lure customers and then raising the price once the firm gains a sound footing. The penetration price will be only for the short term.

Prestige Pricing

Prestige pricing is a pricing strategy whereby the entrepreneur uses higher prices to suggest superior quality and exclusivity. This pricing strategy is often used in the pricing of luxury items and exclusive resorts—items with snob appeal.

Psychological Pricing

Other things being equal, consumers will buy more of a product the lower its price. Psychological pricing is the strategy of setting prices slightly less than a whole number on the premise that customers will focus on the digit that is at the far left. For example, pricing an item at $14.99 instead of $15.00, causes consumers to think of $14.00 rather than $15.00, even though the price is actually closer to $15.00.

Pricing Services

Pricing goods is different from pricing services, and many of the methods of pricing that are used in pricing goods may not apply to pricing services. Here are some methods that can be used in pricing services.

Hourly Rate Pricing

Professionals and skilled technicians often use this method of pricing their services when material costs are not relevant. They establish an hourly rate on the basis of experience, qualification, reputation, or some other consideration. The calculation is relatively simple and straightforward. For example, if a technician values her service at $30.00 an hour, and she spends three hours to repair your device, she will bill you for $90.00, taxes not included.

Retainers

Another popular pricing method used for pricing services is the retainer system. They guarantee you, the entrepreneur, a certain amount of revenue from each client. This makes them rather attractive. Management consultants and other professionals often use this pricing strategy. Their clients sign a contract that entitles them to a given amount of the professional's time.

Flat Fee Pricing

Flat fee pricing, also known as lumpsum pricing, is a pricing method that involves charging a fixed amount of money for a complete job. For example, a carpenter may charge a client $700.00 to build a shed, or a surgeon may charge a patient $2,000.00 to perform a certain operation, or a business consultant may charge $15,000.00 to write up a business plan. If you use this method of pricing, be sure to make allowance for unexpected events such as an increase in the cost of the materials that you use.

BUSINESS CASE 7.2

Roger is accustomed to selling small appliances. To arrive at his prices, he would simply add a certain percentage markup on the cost of the appliances. Now, he has decided to enter the field of small appliance repairs. The problem that Roger now faces is how to price his services because the cost-plus pricing technique does not apply to the appliance repair business.

What advice can you offer Roger to solve his pricing dilemma?

Answer

Roger has learnt that pricing goods is different from pricing services. Whereas the cost-plus method of pricing is applicable to selling small appliances, it does not apply to the small appliance repair business. One pricing technique that Roger might consider is hourly rate pricing whereby clients are charged on the basis of the amount of time the repairs take.

Changing Prices

Prices, once established, will not remain permanently fixed. Cost elements, competitors' pricing policies, supply chain disruptions, consumers' tastes and preferences, and government price regulations are all subject to change, and these changes often require that you change your prices.

Increasing Prices

Other things being equal, an increase in your price will lower the quantity of goods and services that customers will buy from you, but this may increase your profits. A good rule of thumb is, if you are increasing your prices, always explain to your customers why you are doing so. This may serve to strengthen the relationship between you and your customers and increase customer loyalty.

Lowering Prices

You should be reluctant to lower prices because of the tendency among customers to equate low prices with low quality, and you certainly do not want to create a low-quality image for your business. Instead of lowering your prices, you may consider extolling the benefits you offer.

CHAPTER 8

BUSINESS LOCATION

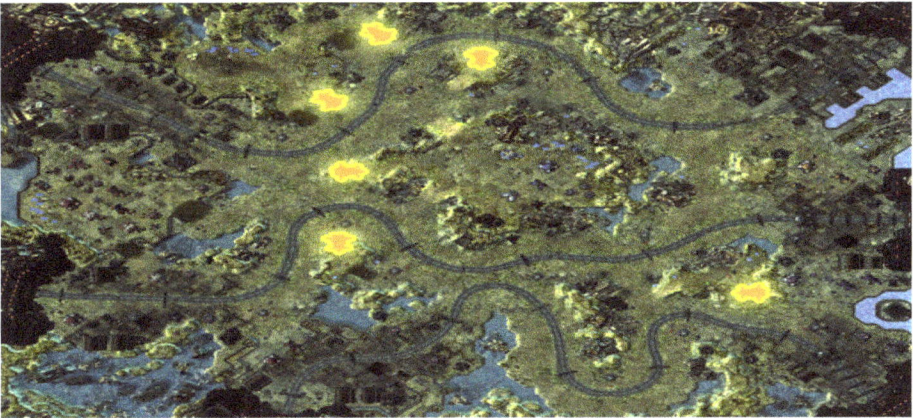

This Photo by Unknown Author is licensed under CC BY-SA

The time will come when you will have to make the important decision about the location of your business.

Introduction

Location, location, location is an expression that is intended to highlight the importance of location to the success of a business enterprise. Bear in mind that a location that may be perfect for a senior citizens' home may be less than ideal for a nightclub. As an entrepreneur, one of the early decisions that you will have to make is regarding the location of your business. In this chapter, we present information that will help you to recognize the importance of location to your business and to choose a location that is appropriate for your business. The topics include the importance of location and home-based businesses.

The Importance of Location

The choice of a location for your business is extremely important for several reasons. Here, we discuss some factors to consider when choosing a business location.

Attracting and Retaining Talents

It is likely that, as an entrepreneur, you will need qualified employees to help with business operations. The location of your business is a prime determinant of the ease with which you are able to attract talent. For example, if your business requires skilled technicians, a city location would be beneficial since it allows relatively easy access to various types of talent. Not only is the location of your business important for attracting qualified employees, but it is also important for retaining them. It is costly to recruit and train skilled workers, hence, it makes good economic sense to retain them. If you are operating from a crummy location, other things being equal, employees will tend to gravitate towards businesses that are operating from more pleasant locations.

Accessibility

In order to have a successful business, customers or clients must be able to reach you either by foot, transportation, or via the internet. No matter how excellent your product or service might be, pedestrian traffic, vehicular traffic, or internet access, are all of vital importance. You must also consider your suppliers. Your business will be better off if they are able to reach you easily. You can easily visualize the problems that would arise if delivery vehicles had difficulty reaching your business. If your business is internet based, the physical location may not be of tremendous importance.

Local Demographics

The story is told of a used (not antique) furniture dealer who wanted to open a store. He did his research to find an area where people were quite wealthy, because he thought that the incomes of potential customers would be a significant determinant of the demand for his product. He was delighted when he found space in an area of town where residents were described as upper income. Gladly, he opened his used furniture store in this upper-income neighborhood. He was utterly dismayed when, after three months of operation, his sales were far below expectation. In this case, the demographics were wrong for this business. High income earners are not likely to buy huge amounts of used furniture. A jewelry store would likely be successful in such a neighborhood.

Cost Consideration

In choosing a location for your business, you must also give serious consideration to cost. Although it may be very desirable to locate your restaurant business, the cost of doing so may be prohibitive. You do not want to spend all your profits on rent.

Infrastructure

Every business, in varying degrees, requires infrastructure to operate. Infrastructure refers to a community's systems of roads, water, power supply, communication, and internet connectivity. The stage of development of the infrastructure of your business location is of utmost importance. It is so obvious that it seems pointless to point out the importance of infrastructure to the successful operation of your business. The nature of your business will help to determine the type of infrastructure that is most important to you and will guide you in your choice of location. A business is a dynamic entity, and a location that was ideal when you first opened the business may now be unsuitable.

BUSINESS CASE 8.1

In selecting a location for your business, the only criterion you need to consider seriously is accessibility. If your clients can reach you easily either by foot or by vehicles, your location problem is solved.

To what extent is the above statement true?

Answer

It is true that the location you choose for your business is of crucial importance, but to suggest that it is the only criterion worth considering is preposterous. It is unnecessary to attempt to rank the criteria in order of importance, but other factors that should be considered are local demographics, cost, and infrastructure.

Home Based Businesses

In discussing business location, we must be aware that many businesses do not need to be concerned with choosing a location, and many of the location factors discussed above may not apply because the business is located at the entrepreneur's place of residence.

Definition of Home-based Business

Before we discuss home-based businesses, let us define precisely what we mean by the concept so that it will be crystal clear what kinds of business operations we are talking about.

A home-based business is a business enterprise that operates from the entrepreneur's dwelling place. It may be a website design business with an office set up in a room at the entrepreneur's house, or it may be a delivery business operating from the owner's garage, or it may be a catering business operating from the caterer's kitchen at home.

We must be careful not to confuse a home-based business with working from home. Depending on the nature of your job, you may not have to report physically to an office, but you perform certain tasks at home. For example, your task today might be to write up a business report. It may be more convenient to work from home on this occasion than to go to the office where you will be subjected to numerous workplace distractions.

Advantages of Home-based Businesses

If you have the option of operating your business from home, you can expect some advantages such as:

- The absence of commuting
- No rental payment
- The convenience of being with family members
- The opportunity to involve family members
- The opportunity to multi-task
- Possible tax benefits

Let us discuss each of the above advantages in turn.

The Absence of Commuting

Commuting from home to work and from work to home, can be quite taxing. Especially if the distance is long, the traffic can take a toll on the commuter. Generally speaking, the time spent commuting is unproductive as far as work is concerned. A home-based business eliminates all the negatives associated with commuting since the home and the workplace are the same.

No Rental Payment

One of the major expense items you will have to face in running a business is rent. Depending on the nature of your business and your location, rent can occupy a significant percentage of your operating expense. The rule of thumb is that you should spend no more than 30% of your income on rent. One of the advantages of operating a home-based business is that you do not have to pay rent, thus you have more money to spend on growing the business.

Being with Family Members

Running a business from home gives you the opportunity to spend more time with family members. When you are at a workplace away from home, your family members just don't have physical access to you for anything. Such is not the case if you are operating a home-based business. In some cases, this is indeed a huge benefit.

The Opportunity to Involve Family Members

If one of your objectives is to involve members of the family in the business, then a home-based business provides an excellent opportunity to do so. If the business operates from the home, family members who are interested can actually see how the business works because the operations are constantly "in their faces." Successors for the business can therefore be assured.

Multi-tasking

A home-based business provides the opportunity to multitask and thus get more things done. There are times in the operation of a business when you are not attending to the business. If the business is away from home, you cannot, for example, do a bit of house cleaning. However, with a home-based business, you can use the time to prepare meals, vacuum the bedroom, or do some garage chores, all while you are at work.

Possible Tax Benefits

Depending on the jurisdiction under which you operate your business, you may be eligible to receive certain tax benefits. Operating your business from home may enable you to claim a portion of your mortgage interest and property taxes. Also, you may be able to write off a portion of your rent if applicable.

Disadvantages of Home-based Businesses

The advantages of home-based businesses are indeed impressive, but that should not blind us to the fact that there are disadvantages as well. Here are some of the disadvantages:

- Distraction of home environment
- Resistance to home-based business
- Lack of business camaraderie
- Disruption of family life

We will discuss each of the above disadvantages in turn.

Distraction of Home Environment

It is undeniable that a home-based business exposes you to a certain level of distraction to which you are unlikely to be exposed in a workplace away from home. Family members vying for your attention, telephone calls that are unrelated to the business, and visitors dropping in are just some of the distractions that you are likely to face when you operate a home-based business.

Resistance to Home-based Business

One of the biggest setbacks of operating a home-based business is some customers just do not feel comfortable going to someone's home for business purposes. The degree of resistance to home-based businesses depends in part on the size of the business and on the type of business.

Customers are likely to show greater resistance to a relatively large bakery business operating from a private home than they would to a small secretarial service operating from a similar place.

Lack of Business Camaraderie

If you enjoy the friendly relationship and mutual trust that is generally associated with a workplace away from home, you will certainly miss them if the workplace is the home. No longer can you meet Jack from Accounting, Mary from HR (Human Resources) and Sally from IT (Information Technology) at the water cooler for hilarious exchanges and office gossip.

Disruption of Family Life

Family members are usually free to do what they want within the confines of their own private home. This may no longer be possible or appropriate where the private home has become the workplace. Certain activities have to be restricted or curtailed in cases where the home and the workplace are one and the same.

BUSINESS CASE 8.2

Jack tries to convince his friend Jill that she could save on income taxes by moving her business from its current location on Main Street to her home. As far as they were able to determine, all other things are equal.

What vital point might Jack be omitting?

Answer

Income tax for a business is a tax on the profits of the business. Jack might be missing the point that whether the business is located on Main Street or at Jill's home, if it makes a profit of $75,000, the income tax is the same. He might be confusing property tax with income tax.

CHAPTER 9

YOUR EMPLOYEES

Entrepreneurs should do their best to hire good employees.

Introduction

There are many entrepreneurs who operate businesses without employees because the volume of work may not require any help. However, it may be absolutely necessary to hire workers in order to keep the business going. Depending on the nature of your business, salaries alone can account for 18 to 52 percent of your operating budget, according to the Society for Human Resource Management (SHRM). Your employees can either make or break your business. It is often said, with more than a grain of truth, that your employees are your most valuable asset.

This chapter deals with your employees. It provides hints pertaining to hiring, conducting job interviews, preparing job descriptions, determining salaries and wages, training, and terminating employees.

Hiring Employees

It is extremely costly to a business to hire the wrong employees. They can be detrimental to the success of your business. The recruiting process is expensive, and so is training. If an employee has to be terminated, of if he or she quits, the business loses its investment in the employee and additional investment has to be made to employ and train a new employee. Here are some guidelines to help you to select the right employees.

1. Select people who are willing to learn and who have analytical skills. Remember that one of the things you are looking for when you hire workers is productivity. That's why you are willing to spend money on training. Money will be wasted on training if the employee is not willing to learn. Employees indicate their willingness to learn by the level of interest they show in the business and by the nature of the questions they ask. Also, employees who are analytical and can see beyond the obvious can make worthwhile contributions to the development of your business.

2. Avoid job-hoppers. Workers, who for one reason or another, have a habit of leaving one job for another, and who show no commitment to their career, should be avoided. In your search for employees, you are looking for people who can contribute to your business on a long-term basis. It is not possible for job-hoppers the offer that kind of commitment.

3. Make sure that the temperament and personality of the employee are consistent with the position for which he or she is being hired. A loner might perform excellently well as an account, but poorly as a part of marketing team. On the other hand, the position of a carpenter who is part of a construction crew might require someone who is a team-player.

4. Pay attention to interns and apprentices. Students on internship, apprentices, and students on job practice can make excellent employees. The advantage of considering this source is that you have an opportunity to observe their work habits to determine their suitability as your employees.

How to Conduct a Job Interview

In most cases, it is advisable to conduct job interviews before hiring employees. This should be an integral part of the selection process. An employment interview is a planned meeting, usually face to face, between a prospective employee and an employer where the employer and the employee have an opportunity to ask and answer questions pertaining to the candidate, the job, and the business.

Bear in mind that the purpose of the interview is to help you to select the employee that is just right for your business. The wrong choice can spell disaster for your business.

Whether the interview is conducted by a single person such as a General Manager or the Manager of the department to which the new employee will be assigned, or by an individual or team from HR, or by some combination of interviewers, the following principles will be beneficial.

Interview Time

Make sure you schedule sufficient time in which to conduct the interview so that you don't have to rush through it. Remember that you are on a fact-finding mission, and you need enough time to pursue clues that may lead to significant revelations. You are also trying to impress the candidate that your company is a good place to work and this also requires time. It is not a good idea to schedule anything really important immediately after the interview because your mind will likely be on that event during the interview and you may lose focus. Note also that you are likely to find out more about the candidate if there is more than one interviewer.

The Interview Location

Conduct the interview at a location that is free from distractions during the interview period so that your attention can be completely focused on the interview. Imagine how distracting it would be if you were to hold the interview in a coffee room where people are constantly coming in and leaving. Telephone calls, incoming and outgoing, should be avoided to the fullest extent possible because they are distracting. The scene is now set for the interview.

Greeting

An employment interview is quite stressful, so it is well to try to make the candidate feel as comfortable as possible, beginning with a warm welcome. If there are other interviewers, introduce them to the candidate. Take this opportunity to explain who you are and your role in the business. Also, explain the roles of the other interviewers in the business, and say a little about the business itself. It's a good idea to outline the process that will be followed.

Asking Questions

A substantial part of the interview involves asking and answering questions. You might have a set of prepared written questions that you plan to ask, but you must be alert and ready to ask follow-up questions based on an answer given by the candidate. The candidate will have his or her own questions. They will likely be about the role that he or she will be expected to play and the business. Make sure that adequate time is available. Look out for candidates who strategically try to spend time on those questions that allow them to emphasize their strengths, thus leaving little or no time to reveal their weaknesses.

Listening Attentively

Listening is closely related to learning, and learning about the candidate and his or her suitability for a position in your business is a matter of prime concern. Sometimes, the entrepreneur is so busy talking and thinking about what next to say that he or she misses most of what the candidate has to say. You have two ears but only one mouth. Maybe that's an indication that you should spend twice as much time listening as you do talking.

It is suggested that the 80/20 rule whereby the interviewer spends 80% of the time listening and 20% of the time talking is a good benchmark for the interview process.

We must be careful not to confuse hearing with listening. Hearing is the ability or the process of perceiving sounds and requires the ears. Listening, on the other hand, is paying careful attention and requires the sense of hearing along with other senses. You can hear the wind whistling through the trees even though you might not be listening. In an interview session, the objective is to hear and listening so that you can learn as much as possible about the candidate.

Be a Salesperson

If, during the interview, you perceive that the candidate might be a good fit for the position, you must be ready to effectively sell the candidate on the position. Point out the merits of the job, and the advantages to the candidate of being a part of the business. Explain how accepting the position could be an opportunity to add value to something worthwhile. Remember that many good employees want to make a significant contribution to society in one way or another.

Note Taking

You cannot always depend on your memory. Just when you need it most, it may fail you. During most interviews, there are important points that are crucial to your hiring decision. Taking notes will ensure that all such points are available to you for the decision-making process. Even though there may be a designated note taker, you should jot down points that you consider to be particularly significant.

End the Interview

At the end of the interview after you have asked all your questions, ask whether the candidate has any questions. After all questions have been answered, inform the candidate what to expect next, such as a call within a day or two, and thank him or her for attending the interview.

After the Interview

While the interview is still fresh in your mind, look at your notes and add any points that you did not have time to jot down during the interview. Reflect on your overall impression of the candidate. If there are other interviewers, discuss the candidate with them. Find out what they consider to be the candidate's strengths and weaknesses. In addition to what you were able to learn about the candidate from the interview session, see what other information you can get from his or her employment record that will help you to make an informed decision. Finally, if you think the candidate is right for the job, make an offer.

The Job Description

After you have hired the employee, you want to make sure that he or she understands what the job entails. A job description is a document that describes the duties and responsibilities associated with a given position. A job description usually contains a job specification which outlines the skills and qualifications necessary to perform the job. Many (perhaps most) job descriptions emphasize the duties to be performed by an incumbent, but job descriptions that emphasize the results to be achieved seem to be very effective. The following is an example of a job description for an Administrative Assistant written in the results-oriented format.

JOB TITLE:	ADMINISTRATIVE ASSISTANT
DEPARTMENT:	OPERATIONS
REPORTS TO:	OPERATIONS MANAGER
JOB(S) SUPERVISED:	OPERATIONS CLERK
JOB PURPOSE:	PROVIDES OFFICE SERVICES TO OPERATIONS
	by
	implementing administrative systems, procedures and policies; monitoring administrative projects.

ESSENTIAL JOB RESULTS:

1. MAINTAINS WORKFLOW

By studying methods; implementing cost reductions; developing reporting procedures.

2. CREATES AND REVISES SYSTEMS AND PROCEDURES

By analyzing operating practices, record-keeping systems, forms control, office layout, and budgetary and personnel requirements; implementing changes.

3. DEVELOPS ADMINISTRATIVE STAFF

By providing information, educational opportunities, and experiential growth opportunities.

4. RESOLVES ADMINISTRATIVE PROBLEMS

By coordinating preparation of reports, analyzing data, and identifying solutions.

5. ENSURES OPERATION OF EQUIPMENT

By completing preventive maintenance requirements; calling for repairs; maintaining equipment inventories; evaluating new equipment and techniques.

6. PROVIDES INFORMATION

By answering questions and requests.

7. MAINTAINS SUPPLIES INVENTORY

By checking stocks to determine inventory level; anticipating needed supplies; placing and expediting orders for supplies; verifying receipt of supplies.

8. COMPLETE OPERATIONAL REQUIREMENTS

By scheduling and assigning administrative projects; expediting work results.

9. MAINTAINS PROFESSIONAL AND TECHNICAL KNOWLEDGE

By attending educational workshops; establishing personal networks; participating in professional associations.

10. CONTRIBUTES TO TEAM EFFORT

By accomplishing related results as needed.

Job Specifications

- A college diploma or equivalent in office management or administrative processes
- Experience in a clerical or administrative position

Career Progression

Progression to Executive Assistant is possible with additional experience and training.

Approved by: _____ **Date:** _____

Day Month Year

_____

Date:_____

Employee's signature

Day Month Year

BUSINESS CASE 9.1

An entrepreneur hires a receptionist and gives her a job description that states, among other things, that her job is to answer the telephone. The telephone rings and the receptionist answers and informs the caller that Miss Simon is not in and hangs up the telephone. She feels satisfied that she has done her job of answering the telephone.

How can the job description be made more effective?

Answer

The receptionist's job description is written in the duty-oriented format in which the duty to be performed is emphasized. The job description can be made more effective by writing it in the results-oriented format. If the job description were to help callers by answering the telephone, the result would be different. The receptionist would have tried to help the caller by perhaps pointing her to someone other than Miss Simon who could help.

Salaries and Wages

The decision regarding the payment of wages and salaries is an important one. Exceedingly high wages attract employees but increase your expenses. Low wages don't attract good talent but may increase your profit margin. In determining what compensation to pay, you must consider wages and salaries that are both fair and competitive. In this section, we discuss briefly the factors that exert the most influence on the determination of wages and salaries.

Qualification and Experience

Other things being equal, the compensation rate is directly related to the employee's level of education and skills possessed. You should expect to pay an employee with an MBA and five years of experience a bigger salary than you would a recent graduate with a bachelor's degree.

The Industry

Some industries traditionally pay higher wages and salaries than others. So the industry to which your business belongs plays a role in what you can expect to pay your employees. For example, a clerk in the health care industry usually earns more than a similar clerk in the food services industry.

The Market for the Particular Talent

The market for the particular talent is a main determinant of the compensation that you will be expected to pay. For example, if a shortage of skilled plumbers exists in your area, then you should expect to pay high wages for the services of plumbers. On the other hand, if there is an exceptionally large amount of bookkeepers who are unemployed in your area, then you might be able to hire one at a relatively low salary.

Location of Your Business

The cost of living differs from location to location, and the cost of living significantly affects wages and salaries. If your business is located in a busy metropolitan area where housing and food and entertainment are expensive, wages and salaries will most likely be quite high. If, on the other hand, your business is located in a rural area where living accommodation and food are cheap, wages and salaries will be comparatively low.

Competitors' Compensation

The factors listed above are all important in determining wages and salaries, but you cannot afford to ignore the compensation that is paid by your competitors. If your wages and salaries are significantly lower than your competitors' wages and salaries, you will not attract good employers. If your wages and salaries are significantly higher than your competitors' wages and salaries, you may be able to attract good workers, but it may negatively affect your profitability. It makes good sense to keep your compensation competitive.

BUSINESS CASE 9.2

Erma declares that it does not matter to her what her competitors pay their clerks, in determining the salaries of her clerks, she uses a simple formula to arrive at what she considers to be a good compensation level. She simply adds 5% on to the minimum wage.

What mistake might Erma be making?

Answer

While adding a markup on the minimum wage might be a relatively simple way of arriving at salaries, it is far from being the generally preferred way. Erma is completely ignoring the need to be competitive. If her salaries are significantly below her competitors', she will not attract highly talented clerks. On the other hand, if her salaries are significantly above her competitors', she could be limiting her profits.

Training

After you have employed your workers, you want to make sure that they contribute as much as possible to the success of your business. You want to ensure that your employees are as productive as possible. This is where training comes in. Training is the process of imparting knowledge and skills to employees to enable them to perform certain tasks effectively and efficiently.

Importance of Training

First, training helps to develop specific knowledge and skills that your business needs to enable you to properly serve your customers. Second, training increases efficiency and reduces cost. Instead of tampering with a piece of equipment and trying to figure out how to use it, training enables you to use it properly to perform the task it was meant to perform. Third, training sends a message to your employees that you value them and are willing to invest in them. It therefore creates employee loyalty. Fourth, training increases job satisfaction because it enables employees to develop confidence in their jobs. Fifth, training goes a long way in reducing employee turnover. Sixth, training increases the quality of customer service and builds customer loyalty which are both highly beneficial to your business.

Terminating Employees

For a multitude of reasons, you may decide that the time has come to part ways with an employee. The termination of employees may be due to any of several reasons, including the following:

- Downsizing
- Inability to perform tasks satisfactorily
- Frequent absenteeism and regular tardiness
- Insubordination
- Noncompliance with company policies and regulations
- Criminal behavior
- Sexual harassment
- Physical violence and verbal abuse in the workplace.

Sometimes it's difficult to end an employer-employee relationship, but you may be left with no choice. Here are a few tips to help you to terminate employees.

1. Make sure that the termination is for just cause. It's a good idea to seek legal counsel on the matter.
2. Let the co-workers know that the employee will no longer be with the company.
3. Inform the employee, face to face, and preferably in the presence of a witness, that he or she is being terminated. Make it clear that the meeting is not a negotiating session and that the decision has already been made.
4. Detail the reason or reasons for the termination, noting that the decision has its basis in fact.
5. Outline any employment benefits to which the employee may be entitled.
6. Outline the procedures for collecting personal belongings and for returning company property.

7. Give the terminated employee an opportunity to ask any questions that he or she may have, and answer them to the best of your ability.
8. End the meeting by thanking the employee for his or her contribution to the business, and wishing him or her the best.

CHAPTER 10

MARKETING

THE MARKETING MIX

This Photo by Unknown Author is licensed under CC BY

Marketing is a business function which, if neglected, can result in business failure.

Introduction

Your business is up and running. You have hired all the help you need, and you are ready to announce to your customers and prospective customers the goods and services that you have to sell. You already have some customers, and they are telling others of the quality of your goods and/or services, but you must now publicize on a broader basis so that your targeted audience will be well-informed and persuaded to patronize your business. Unless people are buying your products in sufficiently large quantities, your business will not be successful. Marketing must be an integral part of your business operation.

The main purpose of this chapter is to acquaint you with this extremely important business function so that you can get maximum benefit from this activity. The focus is on getting your products and services to the intended users—the customers. We will begin the discussion with a definition of marketing. We will then touch briefly on the marketing concept, and marketing functions. Finally, we end the chapter with a discussion of the marketing plan.

Meaning of Marketing

Susan Ward at About.com defines marketing as *"the process of interesting potential customers and clients in your products and/or services."* Realizing the narrowness of this definition, she emphasizes the word "process", noting that marketing involves researching, promoting, selling, and distributing your products or services.

The American Marketing Association (AMA) defines marketing as follows:

Marketing is the activity, set of institutions, and processes for creating, communicating, delivering, and exchanging offerings that have value for customers, clients, partners, and society at large.

Marketing then, would include such activities as:

- Advertising
- Merchandising
- Promotion
- Pricing

- Selling
- Transportation

We define each of these concepts briefly as follows:

Advertising is any paid form of non-personal presentation of ideas or products or services.

Merchandising is the process of selecting, displaying, and promoting products and or services in a distribution outlet.

Promotion refers to various short-term selling efforts including contests, discount coupons, introductory offers and special displays designed to increase sales of a product or service.

Pricing (discussed in Chapter 7) refers to the various strategies used to establish the price of a product or service to make it more appealing to customers.

Selling is the art or technique of personal persuasion employed to convince others to purchase a product or service.

Transportation is the term used for the physical transfer of products from sellers to buyers.

The Marketing Concept

Over time, the concept of marketing has shifted from a product orientation to a sales orientation to a new concept involving a customer orientation, a profit orientation, and an integration of marketing activities.

Customer Orientation

What does customer orientation mean? It means determining what customers want and then allowing those wants to guide the suppliers' activities. From the perspective of the entrepreneur, it means listening to the client or customer and then offering products and services that satisfy the client's or customer's wants and needs. It must be remembered that customers' needs change and the business's ability to meet those needs must also change.

Customer surveys typically reveal the following six basic wants:

- Faster service
- Convenient business hours
- Feeling wanted
- Prompt and fair resolution to problems or disputes
- Product/Service consistency
- Being listened to

Let us examine each briefly.

Faster service Who wants to wait in long lines to be served? Most entrepreneurs recognize that customers have little patience and do not want to wait for an unreasonable length of time to be served. They therefore try to increase their staff and clerical personnel.

Convenient Business Hours People want to conduct their business at times that are convenient to them, and not necessarily when the business place is normally open. This helps to explain to popularity of automated teller machines (ATMs) and extended business hours in many cases. Many business places now open during the traditional lunch hour.

Feeling Wanted People also like to be recognized and treated as being important. Thus, they want to conduct business with people they know or who are respectful. Customer service courses often emphasize the importance of addressing customers by name.

Prompt and Fair Resolution to Problems Many customers complain that some businesses do not handle problems and disputes quickly and fairly. Customers are made to feel at fault, regardless of where the blame actually lies. Many businesses have lost customers because of this failure to resolve customer complaints fairly and promptly. Entrepreneurs who recognize the importance of keeping their customers happy have instituted procedures for settling customers' complaints quickly and fairly. They have reported satisfactory results. A customer-focused business recognizes these wants and takes steps to accommodate its customers. With increased competition in the marketplace, entrepreneurs who pay special attention to their customers will operate at a real competitive advantage.

Product/Service Consistency Product and service consistency is a major building block in creating and maintaining a loyal clientele and customer base. Consistency enables your customers to be confident that they can rely on you to provide goods and services at established and proven standards.

Being Listened To We mentioned earlier that customers like to feel wanted and valued. They also like to be listened to. They know what they want from you in terms of goods and services, and when they voice opinions and concerns, they expect you to listen to them and to respond. This explains why many businesses use suggestion boxes to enable their customers to express their views on the goods and services that they buy.

Profit Orientation

Economists have, for a very long time, assumed that the primary objective of firms is to maximize profits. But profits are generated because firms cater to the needs and wants of customers. Without customers, businesses would have no revenues and no profits. Marketing is directed at protecting and expanding revenue streams. It does so by retaining existing customers, broadening their business relationships by cross-selling products and services, and attracting new customers. Again, without a customer orientation, competitors will entice customers away from you by offering the relationship they desire.

It is important to realize that all customers are not equal, however. They generally fit into one of the following three categories:

- Key customers
- Normal customers
- Problem customers

Key customers are the most profitable. They purchase the highest volume of products and services, and in the case of businesses that offer credit, pay their bills on time and in full. Most customers are *normal customers*. They conduct an average amount of business. The smallest group is *problem customers* who cause the majority of problems. They are slow to honour their contractual obligations, and are chronic complainers. They are most liable to purchase products and return them without a valid reason.

Integration

The new marketing concept emphasizes the coordination of all business activities—new product development, advertising, sales and financial activities. Even before operations begin, the final user is brought into the picture. Information about customers' needs is collected and used to direct operational decisions.

Marketing is the responsibility of every employee. Whether at work or in their leisure time, every employee who comes into contact with a potential or existing customer is marketing the business. Entrepreneurs thus have a responsibility to train employees in terms of how to interact with the public. This focus starts with senior management and the Board of Directors, if one exists, and is equally important for clerks and line personnel.

Marketing Functions

Marketing activities (selling, advertising, transportation, etc.) are contained in six broad marketing functions. Some degree of familiarity with these marketing functions will be useful in marketing your goods and services. The marketing functions are listed below.

1. Market analysis
2. Marketing communication
3. Market segmentation
4. Product differentiation
5. Valuation
6. Exchange

We shall briefly discuss each of these functions in turn.

Market Analysis

The participants in a market are the buyers and sellers. Sellers offer goods and services for sale to customers. Customers want sellers to know what their wants are so that these wants can be satisfied. Entrepreneurs should want to know what their customers and prospective customers want. Market analysis allows entrepreneurs to know who their potential clients are and where they can be found. It also provides much useful on market attractiveness (whether competitors are likely to enter or exit the market), market size in terms of units and dollars, growth of the market (whether expanding or contracting), and profit trends.

Marketing Communication

Information is necessary for good decision making. Marketing communication is the flow of information between customers and the firm. Customers are able to communicate their wants to entrepreneurs who then offer the goods and services to satisfy the expressed needs and wants. Entrepreneurs communicate with potential clients through such means as personal selling, advertising, and publicity. Effective marketing communication involves the coordination of the various communication channels to deliver a clear, consistent, and compelling message about the firm and its products and services.

The main marketing communication tools are:

Advertising: Paid non-personal presentation and promotion of ideas, products, and services by an identified sponsor.

Personal selling: Personal presentation by sales representatives and other members of the firm designed to positively affect sales and strengthen customer relationships.

Sales promotion: Short-term buying motivators aimed at incentivizing buyers to purchase a product or service immediately.

Direct response marketing: A form of direct communication designed to elicit a direct, measurable, and immediate response from a targeted individual or group.

Public relations: the use of favourable publicity to form good relations between a business and the general public, including the firm's clients and prospective clients.

Market Segmentation

An entrepreneur cannot successfully sell its products and services to all people. If you operate a business school, you will be wasting your time trying to sell your services to someone who does not have a car and does not intend to drive one. Your potential clients will be people who want to learn to drive for whatever reason. Similarly, if you own a small real estate business, you will not meet with much success by trying to sell your services to someone who does not have a property and does not intend to own one. In this case, your prospective clients will be people who own real estate assets that they might want to sell and people who intend to purchase real estate.

Entrepreneurs need to identify the segment of the market on which they will concentrate. That is the meaning of market segmentation. Marketing activities will be targeted to particular groups.

The following five standards should be considered when contemplating market segmentation:

1. The market segment should be sufficiently large; otherwise, it might not be profitable.
2. The market segment should be reachable. It should be accessible by the various communication devices and distribution channels that you use or plan to use.
3. The market segment should be identifiable. If the market segment is easily accessible, it will be easier to design a strategy to reach that particular segment. If the segment is not easily identifiable, measurement then becomes difficult, and you will not be able to determine whether it is substantial enough to be profitable.
4. The response of the market segment to particular programs should be different from that of the general population. If all market segments respond in exactly the same way to all stimuli, then there would be no point in targeting any one segment in any special or particular way.
5. The market segment should be stable. If the particular segment is subject to frequent changes, programs designed to reach it will have a high probability of missing the mark.

The following are the main bases for market segmentation.

Demographic segmentation: This involves segmenting the market on the basis of characteristics such as gender, age, income, education, nationality, family size, and ethnicity.

Geographic segmentation: This type of segmentation is based on regions, cities, provinces, states, climate, etc.

Psychographic segmentation: Market segmentation based on lifestyle, values, social status, personality traits, etc. is referred to as psychographic segmentation.

Behavioral segmentation: Behavioral segmentation is based on variables such as price sensitivity, brand loyalty, benefits sought, and rate of use.

Product Differentiation

Product differentiation is the term used to refer to the various methods employed by sellers to make their products or services appear to be different from those of their competitors. If a particular florist were the only one in the market area, there would be no sense in trying to differentiate its product or service. Such a florist would be in a monopoly position. But most entrepreneurs face strong competition. It is to the firm's advantage to be able to be able to convince potential customers that its products and services are different from those of its competitors in ways that will more appropriately cater to their particular wants. The whole purpose is to develop a preference for its products or services.

For a tangible product, product differentiation can be achieved through:

- Distinctive design
- Packaging
- Labeling
- Appearance
- Improving the product by adding desirable features and by increasing its reliability
- Branding
- Improving the availability of the product.

For services, product differentiation can be achieved mainly through quality and pricing. For example, an accounting firm could try to differentiate its services by stressing fast and reliable service, friendliness, and competence.

Valuation

Before a customer decides to do business with a firm, he or she compares the benefits with the costs. Valuation is this process of cost-benefit analysis. Entrepreneurs also engage in valuation. They decide whether the benefits from offering particular products or services are worth the costs. If the entrepreneur can convince the customer that the benefits outweigh the costs, the customer is likely to buy the product or service.

Exchange

The ultimate objective of marketing is to get the customer to use the products or services of the firm—to exchange goods and services for money. The entrepreneur delivers the product or service, and the customer pays for the product or service.

The Marketing Mix

The controllable variables that entrepreneurs will combine (mix) in order to satisfy their customers constitute the *marketing mix*. The marketing mix is usually discussed in terms of the four Ps:

Product

Place

Promotion

Price

Product The firm's product or service must be directly related to its target market. If the products or services offered by the firm do not satisfy the needs of customers, the firm will not be successful.

Place Where and when will customers use the goods and services offered? This is an important question from the point of view of marketing. The products and services must be available at a time and place where customers can obtain or use them. In other words, entrepreneurs must consider the distribution channels to be used in getting products and services to customers. Clearly, this is a more crucial problem in marketing goods than in marketing services, but it cannot be neglected.

Promotion Entrepreneurs must make certain arrangements to communicate with their target market. Prospective clients must have some way of knowing about the firm's products and services. Methods of communicating with potential customers include media advertising, publicity, information brochures, etc.

Price All businesses charge a price for their products and services. In other words, a price is attached to the delivery of products and services. The price must be such that customers will accept it. It must also be such that the business receives adequate compensation for providing the products or services.

It is important to recognize that the four Ps are equally important in the marketing mix. Promotion is not more important than the product because without the product, there is nothing to promote. Neither is the product more important than promotion because unless the entrepreneur promotes the product, it will not reach the customers. A similar equality can be worked out for all the Ps in the marketing mix.

What Is Your Product?

When you enter a hardware store, you know what to expect to find there—nails, screws, tools, plumbing stuff, wheelbarrows, nuts and bolts, door hinges, etc. Similarly, when you enter a grocery store, you know what you expect to find there—rice, cereals, milk, fruit juices, bottled water, fresh and canned vegetables, meat, eggs, cheese, etc. These stores are stocked with scores of merchandise from various producers. They are selling a wide variety of tangible products. You can identify and evaluate these tangible products by their appearance, their shapes, the way they are packaged, and other visible features. The same is not true of services.

BUSINESS CASE 10.1

Peter is convinced that marketing is highly overrated. According to him, an excellent product will sell itself.

Is there anything wrong with Peter's way of thinking?

Answer

Peter is most likely thinking that if the product is excellent, people will buy it. However, that is true only to an extent. We can think of reasons why excellent products may not be sold. The price might be too high, or not enough people know about the product, or people are not aware of its characteristics, or some other reason. Peter needs to understand that marketing involves much more than selling. Activities such as advertising, merchandising, promotion, pricing, and transportation are all aspects of marketing.

Services Are Unique

A law firm, a watch repairer, a building contractor, or a counseling firm is not selling a tangible good; it is selling a service. It is true that in a few cases, the service may be presented in the form of a policy (e.g. insurance) or contract (e.g. lawn care); but the business is selling a service, not a tangible good. The fact that the firm is not selling a tangible product means that many marketing techniques that are effective in marketing goods (tangible products) may be ineffective in marketing services.

Services encompass four unique elements referred to as the four Is of services. These are:

1. Intangibility
2. Inseparability
3. Inventory peculiarity
4. Inconsistency

Let us examine each of these elements briefly.

Intangibility

The element of intangibility that sets services apart from goods (tangible items) presents a challenge for the marketing of services. Since entrepreneurs providing services cannot physically add colour to, change the taste of, or modify the shape of their services, the alternative is to show customers and potential customers the benefits to be derived from using the services. One small business enterprise proclaims its service as "Service you can trust."

Inseparability

In many cases, the customer separates the good from the manufacturer of that good. He or she may not even know who produces the item. In the case of services, the customer identifies the services with the service providers. In the customer's mind, the provider of the service and the service itself are inseparable. This suggests that the entrepreneur's *individual* characteristics will feature significantly in a customer's decision to purchase his or her services.

Inventory Peculiarity

Some goods, such as bananas, fish, and vegetables, are perishable, and others have high storage costs. If a fall in demand results in an undesirable increase in inventory, the producer responds by reducing production and perhaps selling off some of the inventory at reduced prices (an inventory sale). In the case of service businesses, inventory accumulation manifests itself in idle time of employees. The implication for marketing is obvious. For most entrepreneurs in service businesses, inventory cost is very high, so marketing is essential in preventing unplanned inventory accumulation.

Inconsistency

Automation and computerization are two factors that have contributed to the consistency of goods. Whether the quality of goods is excellent, average, or inferior, mass production methods tend to make tangible products consistent. An Epson XP-4200 All-in-one Printer is the same from printer to printer. Of course, there may be one or two defective items in a production batch, but by and large, there will be consistency or standardization.

In the case of services, the same degree of consistency is unlikely. Entrepreneurs' training and experience will tend to reduce inconsistency, but they will not eliminate it. For example, today, the customer service representative is as sharp as a whip, and she solves customers' problems with relative ease. Tomorrow, her performance is not bad, but it is not up to her usual standard. This inconsistency in service makes customers somewhat uncertain as to the quality of service they will receive, and tends to make them reluctant to use the service. Service inconsistency presents a challenge for marketing services.

Marketing Methods

Depending on the nature of your business, you might be able to use many of the following methods to successfully market your product/service. First we list the methods, then we discuss each one.

- Sales letters
- Brochures
- Business cards
- Yellow pages
- Media advertising
- The Internet
- Cold calls
- Guesting on radio and TV

The Sales Letter

Many different types of businesses have successfully used sales letters to attract customers. The effectiveness of the sales letter derives from its ability to be directed straight to its target. If you are aiming at a particular age group, or professional group, or geographical area, the sales letter is a good instrument to hit your target.

Sales letters tend to be most effective when used to sell products or services of a specialized nature, and products/services that are relatively expensive. For example, if your business involves selling computer courses to middle-aged business people in the evenings, you may find the sales letter to be an effective tool. If you operate a retail store, a sales letter informing customers of new arrivals mat help to draw then into your store.

Brochures

Many businesses have built up their customer base by using a brochure. Bear in mind that if you want your brochure to be read, it should be attractive and well laid out. The brochure should have some compelling appearance that provides an incentive for the recipients to read it. There is little doubt that colour enhances the appearance of the brochure, but colour printing is expensive, so you must weigh the benefit of colour against the cost.

If your brochure is massive (more than 25 pages), it probably will not be read as quickly as one that is relatively small and well laid out.

If you decide to use a brochure, it should specify precisely what product or service you are offering, and explain what it is that sets your business apart from your competitors. For a business that is selling a tangible product, the brochure should contain the following information.

- The product that you are offering to your customers. If possible, a brief description should be given
- The benefits to be derived from using your product
- The nature of your price (competitive, below average, etc.)
- Business hours
- Where you are located and/or how you can be reached.

If you are offering a service instead of a tangible product, then your brochure should include the following additional information.

- The service(s) that you offer
- Examples of past work
- Your qualifications and experience
- Special relevant accomplishments

Business Cards

Many entrepreneurs underestimate the value of business cards in marketing their businesses. A business card contains information that customers can use if and when they want your product or service. They seem to be particularly effective for professional and technical service businesses, such as lawyers, consultants, florists, car rental agencies, carpet cleaners, auto mechanics, etc.

The Yellow Pages

Numerous people turn to the Yellow Pages when they want certain products or services. Yellow Page advertising is more effective for some businesses than for others. If you are appealing to a general clientele, then you may want to consider advertising in the Yellow Pages. If you are serving a more specialized clientele, then the effectiveness of yellow-page advertising is questionable.

If you choose to place an advertisement in the Yellow Pages, do remember that larger advertisements tend to be more effective than smaller ones, mainly because people tend to associate small advertisements with small businesses and large advertisements with large businesses. Perhaps you may want to try a large advertisement in the Yellow Pages for one year. If it generates business, then it works. If it does not generate any business, then perhaps you should discontinue the advertisement and simply maintain the usual Yellow Page listing.

Note: *It is worth noting that for many people, especially younger people, the internet has practically replaced the Yellow Pages as a source of information.*

Media Advertising

By media advertising, we mean advertising in newspapers, magazines, trade journals, and radio and television. Most small businesses that advertise use the media. If you know your customers and potential customers, you will have an idea of which media will tend to reach them. A brief discussion of each medium is in order.

Newspapers If you are serving the general public, then a newspaper advertisement may be effective since it will have a large total reach. However, if you are serving a more specialized clientele, then a newspaper advertisement may not reach a sufficient number of your potential customers.

Magazines and Trade Journals If you are serving a specialized group of customers, as opposed to the general public, magazines and trade journals may be good vehicles for reaching your target market. A seller of gardening supplies and equipment could do well by placing an advertisement in a magazine that is devoted to gardening. It would be wise for a computer dealer to place an advertisement in a computer journal.

Radio and Television Radio and television are terrific media for reaching large numbers of people. Their big drawback is that they are expensive. If you decide to use these media, you need to be selective in terms of the times and programs that you choose. You can obtain rate cards from these media that will tell you who listens or watches at what time. Again, if you know your target market as to when your prospective customers are likely to be listening to the radio or watching TV, you could more effectively time your advertisements.

The Internet The Internet is a fantastic medium through which businesses can reach their customers. You can set up your own web site, and there are a number of sites where you can advertise your product or service. The down side is that there are so many businesses on the Internet these days that you run the risk of being lost in the shuffle. It may be worth your while to solicit the help of someone who is knowledgeable about Internet commerce.

One of the advantages of being able to sell your product on the Internet is that you have virtually the whole world as your market. Of course, if you sell via the Internet, you must be prepared to cater to the needs of customers across the globe.

Cold Calls Cold calls are calls made on prospective customers with whom you have had no previous business contact. It involves physically visiting potential customers either where they work or where they live, depending on the nature of your business. Obviously, this method is not appropriate for every business. However, if you use it, you may be able to clinch a sale on the spot. In any event, make sure that you leave your business card and your brochure if you have one.

Guesting on Radio and TV Being a guest on radio and TV gives you exposure and opens up opportunities for promoting your business. This is "free" publicity and if the opportunity arises, you can certainly use it to your advantage. If you have a new product or service, you might be able to interest radio and TV people to have you as a guest.

Evaluative Qualities

In marketing products and services, it is useful to know how customers evaluate their purchases. Tangible products can be evaluated on the basis of color, style, size, shape, etc. The customer can search until he or she finds the items with the desired shape, colour, or size. These qualities of tangible products are referred to as *search* qualities and can be determined prior to purchasing the product.

Certain goods and services such as restaurant meals and haircuts have *experience* qualities that can be determined only during or after the use of the service. In general, services do not possess search qualities. To a certain extent, they possess experience qualities. Mostly, however, they possess what is referred to as *credence* qualities, which are difficult to evaluate. It is often difficult or impossible for a client to determine, whether or not, and to what extent, a small business consultant is offering sound advice. This creates uncertainty in the client's mind and makes it difficult to sell certain services.

What is Your Service?

Earlier in this chapter, we posed the question, "What is Your Product?" It is an important question. Entrepreneurs must have a clear picture of what services they are offering, otherwise, the marketing process will be blurred, a target market will be difficult to identify, and the business may suffer.

BUSINESS CASE 10.2

John Henry is a barber who also sells hair products. He recently launched a marketing campaign for his hair products which, by any standard, must be considered a resounding success. Motivated by the results of his campaign, John decided to launch a similar campaign for his barbering service. It failed miserably.

Why might a marketing campaign that was so successful for hair products fail for barbering services?

Answer

Without knowing the details of the marketing campaign, it is difficult to pin point precisely why it failed for barbering services, but we can hazard a guess as to what might have caused the campaign to fail. The important point to note is that marketing tangible products is different from marketing services. For example, potential customers can see and smell the fragrance of hair products, and marketers can exploit these features. The same is not true of services. The "one size fits all" concept does not apply in this case.

Digital Marketing

It would be a serious omission if we did not pay some attention to digital marketing because it is a means whereby entrepreneurs can really make their businesses successful. Digital marketing, also known as online marketing, E-marketing, or Internet marketing refers to marketing efforts that use the Internet. The use of search engines, and social media such as Facebook and LinkedIn, email, etc. to connect with prospective customers constitutes digital marketing. The prevalence of business websites and social media presence of businesses is evidence of the great importance that entrepreneurs attach to digital marketing.

The Importance of Digital Marketing

Digital marketing has many advantages for the entrepreneur. First, it enables you to reach more potential customers than you can through traditional methods. Second, through digital marketing, you can more precisely target your prospective customers. Third, in many cases, digital marketing is more cost-effective than traditional marketing strategies. Fourth, it allows you to compete more effectively with larger businesses. Fifth, it is relatively easy to change a digital marketing strategy.

It is understandable why so many entrepreneurs turn to digital marketing. However, you must realize that digital marketing does not guarantee success. It must be done properly. If you are not particularly adept at E-marketing, it's a good idea to engage the services of someone who is good at it.

CHAPTER 11

THE MARKETING PLAN

As an entrepreneur, you need a marketing plan to help you achieve your marketing objectives.

Introduction

In a previous chapter (Chapter 4) we discussed the business plan. You may recall that a section of the business plan dealt with marketing. This chapter will examine the marketing plan in significantly more detail. We carefully define the marketing plan, and revisit the marketing mix. We show the importance of the fact book in developing the marketing plan. It might be a good idea to begin by examining the difference between a business plan and a marketing plan.

The Business Plan versus the Marketing Plan

Perhaps the best way to envision the difference between a business plan and a marketing plan, and remove any confusion from your mind, is to view the marketing plan as an integral part of the business plan which guides all aspects of the business so that it can achieve its objectives. The two documents differ in scope. The business plan covers all areas of the business whereas the marketing plan deals specifically with marketing activities that will enable the firm to accomplish its objectives.

Another difference between a business plan and a marketing plan is the time period covered by each document. Whereas the business plan generally covers a period of five years, the marketing plan typically covers a shorter period—one to three years. Somewhat related to the time period covered is the frequency with which the plans are updated. Business plans are updated generally when a significant event such as the adoption of a new business model is adopted. Marketing plans are updated less frequently, typically yearly with the budgeting process.

Definition of the Marketing Plan

From the previous section, you may have some idea of what a marketing plan is, but it seems to be a good idea to formally define it. A marketing plan is a document that outlines in some detail, the strategies that a business will use to achieve its marketing objectives.

Quite often, no distinction is made between a marketing plan and a marketing strategy because the marketing plan consists of the firm's overall marketing strategy. Both emphasize the firm's value proposition which is the feature that makes the firm or its goods and services attractive or appealing to its customers.

The Marketing Mix Again

When developing a marketing plan or a marketing strategy, firms normally focus on the marketing mix—product, place, promotion, and price. These factors define the total relationship between a firm and a particular customer. The basic element of a product or service is the benefit that a customer expects to realize: transaction convenience from online applications, for example. Physical distribution (place) refers to the process by which a business delivers the product or service to the customer. This may be a client card, or electronic transaction using a computer. Promotion refers to the types of activities employed by a business to communicate with customers regarding a product or service. Advertising and publicity attempt to increase the demand for the underlying good or service. Pricing decisions, of course, influence the quantity demanded and relative profitability to the firm.

BUSINESS CASE 11.1

The existence of a marketing plan is a sign that the business plan is lacking in certain respects.

What is wrong with the above statement?

Answer

It seems as if the statement is implying that the marketing plan is a document contained within the business plan. To a certain extent, this is true. Elements of the marketing plan are contained in the business plan, but details of the firm's marketing activities in its entirety, are contained in an independent document that we refer to as the marketing plan.

Your Marketing Plan

Your marketing plan is the document that sets forth how you intend to reach your desired goal. Without it, there is a high probability that you will find yourself in an undesirable position that is some significant distance away from your desired goal.

The Fact Book

The fact book or fact sheet is a document that contains pertinent background information about the industry of which the firm is a part. With this information, it becomes relatively easy to prepare the marketing plan. The facts contained in the fact book or fact sheet include:

- Market information
- Customer/client information
- Marketing information
- Financial information

Market information includes variable such as market size in unit volume and dollar value, competitors' sales in units and dollar value, and competitors' market share.

Customer information includes variables such as age, gender, education, and income. It also includes information about where and when they buy, where they live, family size, and their marital status.

Marketing information includes advertising activities in the industry and by particular firms (including samples of advertising messages), sales promotion strategies, and public relations activities.

Financial information includes product and service pricing strategies and structure, profit information, and budget figures.

Given the strategic importance of the marketing plan, you should give careful consideration to its preparation. The following steps should guide you through the process. Like the business plan, the preparation of a marketing plan requires a certain amount of expertise. If necessary, do get some assistance in preparing your marketing plan.

Step 1. Situational Analysis

This step in the market planning process requires a description of the circumstances surrounding your decision to own and operate a small business. Perhaps, for example, you saw an opportunity to satisfy a particular need. This section of the marketing plan should also describe present market conditions, including any possible marketing opportunities that may present themselves in the future. The situational analysis should contain information on the size of the market, its growth rate, its demographic features, pertinent government regulations, and competitive factors.

Step 2. Target Market Identification

In this section of the marketing plan, you specify the segment(s) of the market that you propose to serve. In part, the nature of your business will help to determine your market segment. For example, if your business is a hardware store, your target market would probably be tradespeople, home owners and maintenance workers.

Step 3. Identifying Strengths and Weaknesses

Having identified your market segment, you must then identify strengths and weaknesses in your product/service. A strength of your business could be the ability to serve customers quickly. A weakness could be lack of resources to expand the current business into other areas.

Step 4. Goal Setting

The next step in the process is the establishment of goals. These goals should be expressed in concrete terms. For example, instead of stating a goal as an increase in profits, it is preferable to state it in more concrete terms such as increasing profits by 10% over the previous year. Your goals could include increasing your customer base by 20% by the end of the next year, increasing your total revenues from repairs by 15%, or adding a new service by a specific date. Remember that your goals and objectives should be SMART (specific, measurable, attainable, realistic, and timely).

Step 5. Action Plan

In this section of your marketing plan, you outline the strategy that you will use to achieve your marketing objectives. For example, a strategy could be an increase in your advertising budget by 15% in order to increase your customer base by 10%.

Step 6. Assignment of Responsibility

Here, you specify who will be responsible for the implementation of the marketing plan. The relevance of this step depends on the size of your business establishment. If you are the only one in your firm, then the responsibility will fall squarely on your shoulders. If there are others in the business, such as partners or employees, then the task should be assigned to someone who has the ability to perform the task.

Step 7. Budgeting

In this section of the marketing plan, you explain the allocation of funds to the various marketing activities. If financial resources are inadequate to allow for the implementation of the marketing strategy, then the plan may have to be modified or additional resources will have to be found.

Step 8. Progress Evaluation

The marketing plan is designed to help you accomplish certain objectives in a specified period of time. You must evaluate the progress of your marketing efforts in order to determine the success of the plan. This type of monitoring allows you to make any adjustments that may be necessary.

A Final Warning

A word of caution is in order. There are many pre-designed computer packages containing ready-made marketing plans. There are also many business experts who can prepare a marketing plan on very short notice. A marketing plan is a plan to market *your* business and *your* products/services. It should therefore be specific to your particular business, and you should have a significant input in its preparation. Too many marketing plans fail because they were unrelated to the business they purported to guide.

BUSINESS CASE 11.2

As long as a business enterprise is accomplishing its marketing goals as set out in its marketing plan, we know that the business is definitely operating effectively.

What are your thoughts on this statement?

Answer

It is indeed a good (maybe even great) thing for a business enterprise to accomplish its established marketing goals. However, we must remember that as important as these marketing goals may be, there is more to a business than achieving marketing goals. What about its human resources, for example? Are employees motivated? Is the business profitable? Is it comfortably managing its financial obligations? The point being made here is that a business is made up of different components, and the proper functioning of all is required for business success.

Marketing Plan Contents

There is no strict rule about the format of a marketing plan. Table 11.1 shows the contents of a marketing plan for a hypothetical small business enterprise.

Table 11.1 Contents of a Marketing Plan

1. Executive Summary
A. Business Overview
B. Product/Service Strategy
C. Market Analysis
D. Marketing Plan

11. The Business
A. Business Description
B. Vision and Mission

111. Situation Analysis
A. Industry Analysis
B. Market Environment
C. Pricing and Profitability
D. Customers

1V. Product/Service Strategy
A. Current Products/Services
B. Research
C. Operations
D. Procedures

V. Market Analysis

A. Market Segments

B. SWOT Analysis

C. Competition

D. Risk

V1. Marketing Plan

A. General Marketing Objectives

B. Marketing Communication

C. Sales Strategy

D. Distribution Channels

E. Advertising and Promotion

F. Public Relations

CHAPTER 12

PROTECTING YOUR ASSETS

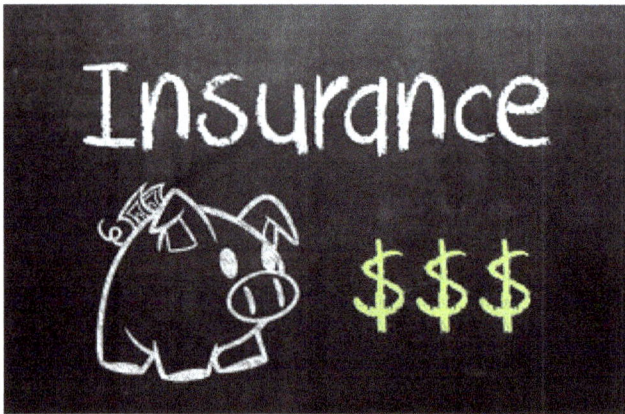

This Photo by Unknown Author is licensed under CC BY

Smart entrepreneurs protect their assets by purchasing adequate insurance.

Introduction

Whether your business enterprise operates as a single proprietorship, a partnership, or a corporation, it is good business sense to protect your assets. By practising the principles that we have expounded in this book, you will, indirectly, be protecting your assets.

Entrepreneurs are, by definition, risk-takers, and the profits they earn are the reward for risk-taking. As an entrepreneur, your business is exposed to a variety of risks such as:

1) the risk of increased competition from new entrants into your market

2) the risk that the growth of your entire industry may slow down, thus affecting your small business negatively

3) the risk that the economy may experience a recession, thus reducing your customers' ability to purchase your product/service

4) the risk of fire, flood or other catastrophic occurrences, and

5) the risk of government legislation that may adversely affect your business.

This chapter shows you how you can take direct measures to safeguard your business assets. In many cases, by protecting your business assets you will be protecting your personal assets as well.

Business Risks

The list of risks that your business faces extends far beyond the short list given above. You may be surprised at the extent of risk involved in running a business. If you are not familiar with these risks, you will be unprepared to deal with them, and you could end up losing your business and personal assets. Consider how each of the following occurrences would affect your business enterprise.

(a) Fire destroys your office furniture and equipment.

(b) A thief breaks into your office and takes off with your computers, photocopy machine, fax machine and other office equipment.

(c) A hurricane or a tornado damages your business property to the amount of $100,000.

(d) Your delivery vehicles are severely damaged by vandalism.

(e) Your office leaks during a heavy rainfall and causes severe damage to your furniture and important documents.

(f) One of your employees sustains a severe injury while at work.

(g) One of your customers injures his/her leg after tripping over an extension chord on your premises, and is awarded a liability judgement of $10,000

(h) You lose your business partner through sudden death.

(i) You sustain substantial financial loss because of shoplifting.

(j) You extend credit to many of your customers and thus suffer substantial loss because of bad debts.

Dealing with Risk

The most effective way of dealing with the various forms of risk that your business may face is to institute a risk management program. Risk management involves plans to deal with potential losses *before* they occur. Instituting a good risk management program entails the following:

- Identification of potential losses
- Planning to deal with the potential losses identified
- Regular revision of the risk management program.

Identification of Potential Loss

The risks to which your business is exposed must be identified before you can effectively deal with them. These potential losses may be classified as direct losses, such as property damage by fire; indirect losses, such as loss of revenue due to damaged equipment; liability losses, such as losses due to claims or lawsuits against your business; and human resource losses, such as the death of one of your business executives.

Planning to Deal with Potential Losses

Once you have identified your exposure to loss, the next step is to decide how you will deal with the potential losses. Essentially, you will have four options: avoid the risk, transfer the risk, assume the risk, or reduce the risk of loss.

Below, we will discuss good management as a way of avoiding risk and reducing the risk of loss. Assuming the risk involves setting aside money to take care of losses when they occur. Risk assumption is itself risky and not advisable for most small businesses. Instead of laying aside huge sums of money to provide for losses, it may be more practical to transfer the risk by means of insurance. We will discuss insurance as a way of transferring risk.

Revision of the Program

The potential losses to which your business is exposed will vary from time to time. As an entrepreneur, you must regularly review and update your risk management program. For example, the introduction of a new business activity could very well expose you to additional risk, and new legislation and regulations may necessitate changes in your risk management program.

Good Management and Insurance

Even the extended list of possible losses given earlier in this chapter is inadequate to cover the numerous risks that businesses face. Fortunately, you are not totally defenseless in terms of coping with these risks. As indicated above, you can deal with many of these risks by instituting a good risk management program. In many cases, you can minimize or even eliminate many of the risks. Let us consider good management and insurance as ways of dealing with risk.

Good Management

A good financial plan will enable you to anticipate capital needs, help you to secure proper financing, examine the movements of certain key financial variables, and thus avoid financial difficulties. A good marketing plan will help you to carefully study the market for your product/service, study the effect of competition on your business, and provide a suitable reaction to your competitor's moves. These are all aspects of good management that will reduce risks.

By practising good business management, you will be able to avoid or minimize the impact of many of the risks that your business may face. For example, it is well known that shoplifting is responsible for a large part of the losses sustained by many business enterprises. Some entrepreneurs respond to this situation by raising prices to counteract the loss from shoplifting. This often has the effect of reducing sales, while not reducing shoplifting. Good management would involve the installation of electronic cameras and/or the hiring of security guards both to deter and detect shoplifters.

Theft by employees has caused many businesses to bite the dust. Theft by employees runs the gamut from taking home small items such as pens, pencils, computer parts, calculators, towels, chocolate bars, and small car parts from the workplace to stealing time by arriving late for work and leaving before the scheduled closing time. When such events occur with considerable frequency, they exact tremendous costs on the business. If you suspect that your workers are stealing, then policies should be put in place to check employees before they leave at the end of the work day. An effective system for checking in and checking out workers to ensure that they deliver a full day's work is just good management.

Good management can also prevent or minimize loss that is due to poor credit practices. If your business extends credit, make sure that you know the customers to whom you are extending credit by having them fill out a credit application form from which you will gather information such as name of customer, address, date of birth, employment, present salary, bank information, credit references, etc. It might surprise you to know that many entrepreneurs have extended credit to customers whose faces they know only from the fact that they have been frequent patrons. Ensure also, that you run an appropriate credit check before you grant credit.

Do you have a sprinkler system installed? Do you keep proper functioning fire extinguishers on your premises? Have you installed an alarm system? Do employees in your factory wear hard hats for safety? Do you carry out safety checks on your vehicles? Have you secured the entrance to your business premises to make unwanted forced entry difficult? Do you have fire drills periodically? These questions indicate steps that you can take to reduce risk and avoid losses. They are a part of what constitutes good management.

Insurance

Insurance enables you to transfer risks and thus effectively safeguard your business assets from losses that can result from many of these risks. It is a smart decision to use insurance to minimize your losses. The importance of insurance becomes evident when you consider what would happen to your business enterprise if you were found liable for a substantial sum without relevant insurance coverage.

Claims against you or your business can be a tremendous set back to any business owner who is not adequately protected by insurance. To operate your business enterprise without any kind of insurance at all is, to put it bluntly, to flirt with disaster.

Types of Insurance Coverage

There are many types of insurance coverage, and insurance brokers and agents are ready and eager to sell you any of a variety of insurance. It does not make good economic sense to attempt to insure your business against every conceivable risk. The premiums that you would have to pay would exceed the benefits from such coverage. However, in buying insurance coverage, you should consider, in addition to the protection of your assets, the peace of mind and freedom from worry that insurance provides.

The type of insurance that you will need depends on the nature of your business. An accountant operating out of a small business office with only a secretary would probably need less insurance than a small manufacturer with 10 employees, factory equipment, and a few delivery trucks.

Typically, an entrepreneur would consider the following types of insurance:

Property

Liability

Theft, Robbery and Burglary

Protection of Property The main type of insurance in this category is probably fire insurance. Depending on the jurisdiction, a standard fire insurance policy may insure you only for fire, lightning, and losses resulting from the temporary removal of assets from your office because of fire. This basic coverage may be broadened by endorsements to include landslides, falling objects, broken glasses, broken water and heating systems, and other such damages to property.

Liability Insurance If a receptionist, a designer, a clerk, or some other employee in your business is injured because of negligence or carelessness on your part, you may be liable for damages. Workers' Compensation may be applicable in some jurisdictions. You will be able to protect yourself against liability for injury to your employees while they are engaged in their duties.

You are responsible for injury or damage to persons or property of others that is due to your negligence. You can protect yourself against damage claims brought against you by purchasing liability insurance. A policy may be arranged to cover all liability risks in connection with the operation of your business, subject to a few exclusions. If you do not require such a comprehensive liability policy, you can obtain one that is tailored to your specific needs. For example, you could obtain a policy that covers tenants' liability, professional liability, and contractual liability.

Theft, Robbery, and Burglary Insurance *Theft* is defined as the stealing of your property. If someone steals your fax machine while it is unprotected, the loss is classified as theft. *Robbery* entails depriving you of your property by violence or the threat of violence. If you were just about to leave your office to go to your bank to make a deposit, and someone holds you up at gun point and relieves you of your cash, such a loss would be classified as robbery.

Burglary is the forcible entry of your premises. If someone breaks down the door to your store, and steals your merchandise, or your furniture and equipment, that loss would be classified as burglary. Clearly, these losses can seriously affect your business enterprise. Insurance can provide protection against such losses.

BUSINESS CASE 12.1

The Lawn Greene is a hypothetical lawn mowing business owned and operated by Joe Greene. Joe is a very careful entrepreneur who has a relatively low tolerance for risks. The Lawn Greene owns a fleet of lawnmowers and other tools such as hedge trimmers and rakes. Joe employs six other people to help to run the business. To fully protect his business, Joe has wasted no time in securing property and theft, robbery, and burglary insurance.

What major type of insurance might Joe be overlooking?

Answer

Joe needs to seriously consider liability insurance. This will protect him from liability for injury to his employees while they are engaged in their duties, and also from liability for injury to clients or visitors to Lawn Greene.

Life Insurance

The fact that we have not said much about life insurance should not detract from its importance for your business enterprise. The truth is, you may find life insurance quite useful for your business. In certain circumstances, a lender may require that you take out a term life insurance policy as a pre-requisite to obtaining a loan. You may be able to attract and keep good employees through the establishment of a group life insurance, and a private pension plan through an insurance company. Other types of life insurance might be of interest to entrepreneurs. It may be well worth your while to pursue the matter of life insurance and how you may use it as a business owner.

Understand Your Policy

This author can recount numerous cases where entrepreneurs believed that they were covered from certain losses, only to be surprised to find that when a claim was made, they were told that their policy did not cover such and such. The actual policy might state something quite different from what the insurance agent tells you. Read the so-called *fine print*. Insurance policies often contain terms and phrases that are unfamiliar to the typical entrepreneur. If you don't understand your policy, get help from a lawyer.

A Final Word on Insurance

In this chapter, we have drawn your attention to what we consider to be some relevant aspects of insurance. Insurance is a very complex matter and we have attempted to make you aware of what insurance can do for your business in terms of protecting your assets.

We have examined only a small fraction of the various types of insurance. It is unlikely that you will need all the different types of insurance that are available, or that you will be able to afford them if you wanted them. Since insurance costs money, and since you do not have unlimited financial resources, choosing the types of insurance that are of greatest importance to your business operation is a matter that requires you to exercise good judgement.

The careful planning and selection of insurance is a necessary step in managing a business for success. Adequate protection by insurance coverage significantly reduces the risk of business failure, relieves you of needless worry and gives you peace of mind. It allows you to focus more on satisfying your customers' needs.

BUSINESS CASE 12.2

An insurance agent is making a huge effort to convince Joe, the proprietor of Lawn Greene, to buy life insurance. Joe insists that he cannot see how his business can possibly benefit from life insurance.

How might the agent convince Joe that life insurance can benefit Lawn Greene?

Answer

Obtaining life insurance to benefit a business seems counterintuitive since a business is not a person. That probably explains why Joe is not responding positively to the insurance agent. Maybe the agent would have better success by pointing out to Joe that life insurance could help him to obtain financing for Lawn Greene. Also, group life insurance could attract better employees.

CHAPTER 13

CREDIT SELLING

Credit selling is an excellent way to boost sales.

Introduction

When I was a boy, I recall going into a small village shop. Just over the counter, in black bold letters was a sign that read:

"Trust is dead. Bad pay killed him."

Not very far from that sign was another which read:

"I have credited but to my sorrow, so buy today and credit tomorrow."

There was no doubt in my mind then that this particular shopkeeper had absolutely no interest in credit selling. Having read those signs, customers knew better than to request credit.

Today, we live in a different world – a world in which credit in business is almost as normal as going to school. The fact is, credit selling increases sales volume. This, of course, is tremendously attractive to entrepreneurs who are interested in increasing their profits, because profits depend on total sales revenue and total cost. Recall the equation defining profits:

$$\textbf{Profit = Total revenue} - \textbf{Total cost.}$$

Notwithstanding the popularity of credit in today's business world, many entrepreneurs still do not extend credit privileges to their customers. That is because there are certain risks involved in extending credit. For example, the customers may not honour their obligations to pay or they may fail to make the agreed-upon payment at the specified time. In this chapter, we will examine the use of credit sales by entrepreneurs. In particular, we will pay some attention to the various types of credit, credit management, and credit cards.

Types of Credit

There are two main types of credit that small businesses entrepreneurs may extend to their customers. They can establish charge accounts (also called open account credit), or they can arrange to accept credit card purchases. Customers who make credit card purchases must first be approved for credit by a credit card company, therefore the risk to the business offering that kind of credit is substantially reduced. We will pay more attention to credit card use by entrepreneurs later in this chapter. Now, we turn our attention to charge accounts.

Charge Accounts

A customer enters a bar owned by a single proprietor. He sits and orders a drink. In 10 minutes, he orders another drink as he engages in trivial discussions with other patrons. Finally, he gets up to leave, telling the bartender, "Charge it to my account." He is able to do that because he has established a charge account at that particular business establishment. The amount of the sale will subsequently be recorded on the books of the establishment. All such charges by this customer will be totaled and entered on a statement that will be sent to the customer at a certain time of the month. Until the bill is paid, it appears on the balance sheet of the establishment as accounts receivable. Clearly, slow payment or non-payment by charge-account customers can create a serious cash flow problem for the business owner.

Benefits and Costs

If businesses did not derive any benefits from extending credit to their customers, it is doubtful that they would engage in that activity. It has been established that charge customers buy much more than cash customers at any given business establishment where credit selling exists. There seems to be something in the psychology of buyers that favors credit buying over cash buying. Even in cases where customers can comfortably make cash purchases, they seem to opt for credit purchases.

From the point of view of the firm, extending credit to customers increases their purchasing power, thus making it possible for them to purchase more of the firm's products. Also, many customers find it more convenient to use credit than to use cash for a variety of transactions. For these reasons, extending credit has the benefit of increasing sales.

If the benefits derived from extending credit were attainable without cost, all businesses would engage in credit selling. But there are many businesses that sell only on a cash basis. This suggests that there are certain costs associated with credit selling and that these costs may even outweigh the benefits. Many entrepreneurs have embarked on an unsound policy of credit extension. To their own detriment, they had failed to consider the costs involved. What exactly are these costs? Let's investigate.

What additional costs are you likely to incur if you establish charge accounts? Here are some of them. First, the establishment of charge accounts requires additional record-keeping to keep track of credit sales and customers' indebtedness to your business. This means time and money. Second, there are stationery costs in the form of envelopes, invoice forms, letterheads, credit application forms, etc. Third, there is the cost of postage. This can be considerable if you have a large number of charge customers. Let's assume that you are a business owner and that you have an average of 100 statements to send out each month to your charge-account customers. During the course of one year, you will spend a considerable amount on postage alone. Fourth, you may incur credit collection costs in the form of collection letters, probably written by your lawyer, and charges from collection agencies if the accounts have to be turned over to a collection agency for collection. Finally, once you decide to extend credit, there will be some bad debts that will never be paid.

These costs have deterred many entrepreneurs from extending credit. But the prospect of increased sales is often too tempting for some to ignore. What is required is a good credit-management program if you are to take advantage of the opportunities for increased sales made possible by credit selling.

Credit Management

When you extend credit, you do so with the belief that the account will be paid at some stipulated future date. If, not, there would be no logical business reason to extend credit. Before you extend credit, you must take certain precautions to reduce the risk of nonpayment. The fact is, some customers are simply bad credit risks. You must set up a system that will preclude the granting of credit to such customers. Even your regular customers may turn out to be unworthy of credit.

Large institutions that regularly grant consumer credit often use rather sophisticated models to help them evaluate the creditworthiness of the customer. You may not have access to such elaborate means of evaluating your customers, nevertheless, it is foolish to simply grant credit to everyone who requests it.

In order to insulate yourself against bad credit risks, you should take the following steps:

1. Collect basic relevant information about the applicant. Relevant information would include the following:
a) customer's name
b) customer's current address
c) age
d) marital status
e) number of children
f) employment status, including name of employer and length of employment
g) take-home pay
h) creditors
i) bank information

This information can conveniently be collected by having the applicant fill out an appropriate credit application form.

2. Collect information about the applicant's credit record. There are credit bureaus in most large cities. These and other credit agencies are good sources of credit record information.

3. Establish a credit limit. This should be based on the applicant's ability to pay as revealed by the data collected in numbers 1 and 2 above. It is a good idea to be conservative in establishing the credit limit. This limit may be increased in the future after the customer has demonstrated greater creditworthiness. If the information reveals that the applicant is a bad risk, then credit should be refused. If you must refuse an application for credit, explain the reason for the decision and point out to the applicant that you feel it is in his/her best interest that credit not be extended at this time.

4. Carefully monitor all charge accounts, especially new ones, and take appropriate measures to deal with accounts that are in arrears. You should cut off credit from customers who are continually delinquent in settling their accounts, informing them that you will be ready to resume the credit relationship with them in the future when their conditions improve.

No matter how well you manage your charge accounts, some accounts will still be delinquent and others will be uncollectible. When you must cancel the credit privileges of customers, you may lose them forever. Good credit management involves dealing with delinquent accounts in such a way as to minimize your losses while at the same time trying to maintain a cordial relationship with the customer.

When an account becomes delinquent, send a friendly reminder. This could state that you believe that it was an oversight that has caused the account not to be paid. Include the original invoice and ask for payment. The reminder could include a statement asking the customer to contact you if there is a problem. It is better to arrange easier payment terms that are manageable than not to collect at all.

If you do not receive a response within a reasonable time (about 10 days), then contact the customer by telephone, and inquire why payment has not been made. Try to find out when the customer intends to make payment. If you still do not receive the promised payment, send a letter indicating that the customer's credit standing is in jeopardy and that the account will be turned over to a collection agency or your lawyer in a certain number of days.

If there is no response by the stipulated date, send a registered letter informing the customer that the account is being referred to your lawyer or a collection agency.

This method is clearly time-consuming and expensive. It may cause irreparable damage in the relationship between you and the customer, and it may not be particularly good for public relations. This simply highlights the importance of carefully screening applicants before granting credit.

BUSINESS CASE 13.1

When the Corner Shop opened some years ago, it had a "no credit" policy. As time passes, many of its customers began to ask for credit. The owner, George, eventually relented and began to offer credit. Shortly thereafter, goods flew off the shelves, but receipts fell because of failure on the part of customers to pay their bills. George quickly returned to his "no credit" policy.

What could George have done to enable him to benefit from extending credit to his customers?

Answer

George could have benefited from credit sales by instituting credit management in his shop. Prior to extending credit, George could have collected relevant information on customers applying for credit so that they could have been screened to determine their creditworthiness. This would not necessarily eliminate bad debts but it would definitely reduce it.

Credit Cards

Because of the costs and problems involved in establishing and managing charge accounts, many entrepreneurs consider that the costs of charge accounts outweigh the benefits, and hence do not extend credit as a rule. Their position is understandable. Entrepreneurs can use credit cards as a way of financing some of their expenses. Here, we show how business owners can use credit cards to boost their sales.

The acceptance of credit card sales avoids many of the problems associated with charge accounts. Today, customers use credit cards widely. Can you think of a service station or a restaurant or a clothes boutique that does not honour any credit cards? Credit card sales have become so popular that many merchants now indicate which credit cards they accept by posting notices (usually the sign of the card) on the entrance to their business places.

In order to accept credit card purchases, you must first make arrangements with the credit card company. There is a charge based on the amount of credit card sales. The mechanical details of credit card transactions need not detain us here. Suffice it to say that entrepreneurs are making increasing use of sales by credit cards.

In spite of the credit card company charge, businesses still find it worth their while to opt for credit card sales over charge accounts. They seem to believe that the costs of establishing and managing charge accounts outweigh the credit card company charge. This is evidenced by the obvious movement away from charge accounts and toward credit card selling. With the increasing popularity of credit cards among consumers, more and more businesses will conduct transactions by accepting credit cards.

BUSINESS CASE 13.2

Mark was shocked to find out that his friend Deon did not accept credit card payment at her counseling business. Mark carefully pointed out to Deon all the benefits that she could derive from accepting credit cards. When asked about the downside, Mark assured her that there were none.

Was Mark right?

Answer

Mark was quite right when he pointed out that there were benefits to be derived by accepting credit card payments. However, Mark was wrong in stating that there was no downside. If Deon decides to accept credit card payments, she will incur additional costs in the form of set-up fees, as well as card processing fees which, over time, can be significant. Moreover, accepting credit card payments involves additional work and expense in setting up and maintaining extra bookkeeping system. Additionally, accepting credit card payment exposes Deon to additional risk in the form of fraudulent card use which can have serious negative consequences.

GLOSSARY OF
COMMON BUSINESS TERMS

✦

This glossary of common business terms provides a convenient reference for the entrepreneur. It contains many of the terms found in the book, but it also contains many business terms that are not mentioned in the book.

Accelerated depreciation: depreciation at a rate faster than usual.

Accident insurance: a policy that allows for payment of a stipulated sum in the event of injury or accidental death.

Account: a statement showing debit and credit entries.

Accountant: a trained professional who analyses and reports business or organizational financial transactions.

Accounting: the process of recording and analyzing financial information. The principles and procedures of recording, summarizing, and reporting financial transactions.

Accounts payable: amounts owed by a business because of normal business transactions. An example would be unpaid bills for supplies.

Accounts receivable: amounts owing to a business because of normal business transactions. An example would be the amount due to a business for credit sales.

Accrual basis: a system of allocating revenue and expense items on the basis of when the revenue is earned or the expense incurred rather than when the cash is received or paid out.

Acid test ratio: the ratio of cash assets to current debts.

Act of God: an event such as hurricane or natural flood that is beyond human control.

Ad valorem: based on value rather than on weight. For example, an ad valorem tariff is one that is based on the value of the item rather than on its weight or quantity.

Advertising: any paid form of nonpersonal presentation and promotion of goods or services.

Agent: one who acts on behalf of another in transactions with a third party.

Alien corporation: a corporation doing business in one country but chartered in another.

Amalgamation: the merging or integration of two or more business concerns.

Amortize: to reduce or liquidate by installment payments.

Annual report: a report prepared for delivery at the end of the fiscal year about the financial transactions of an entity.

Annuity: a series of payments over a specified number of years.

Appraisal: the process of evaluating an employee's job performance.

Appreciation: an increase in value over a period of time.

Arbitration: the process of settling disputes between two parties by an impartial third party.

Arm's length: transactions between parties who are not related.

Arrears: payments that are past due.

Articles of incorporation: legal documents pertaining to the incorporation of an entity.

Asset: anything of value that is owned by an entity.

Audit: an official inspection of an entity's operations.

Bad debt: money owed to you that you are unlikely to collect.

Bait and switch: a deceptive sales practice whereby a customer is attracted by advertisement of a low-priced item but then is encouraged to purchase a higher-priced one.

Balance sheet: a statement of assets and liabilities on a specific date.

Balloon payment: a final lump sum payment made to liquidate a financial obligation.

Bank rate: the rate of interest that the central bank charges on loans to commercial banks.

Bankruptcy: a state in which an entity is unable to pay its debts.

Bear market: a market in which prices are falling.

Bill of sale: a certificate of transfer of property from one owner to another.

Blue chip: a term used to describe stocks or companies that are of high quality.

Bond: a certificate of indebtedness of the issuer to the holder.

Book value: the value of an asset as recorded on the company's books.

Brand: a mark (trade-mark) that identifies a product.

Break-even point: the point at which total revenue is equal to total cost so that profits are just zero.

Broker: one who brings a buyer and seller together for a fee or commission.

Budget: a plan for future revenues and expenditures during a specified period of time.

Bull market: a market in which prices are rising.

Burglary: forcible entry to take property unlawfully.

Business cycle: ups and downs in business conditions over a period of time.

Business model: an explanation of how a business plans to earn a profit.

Business plan: a carefully drafted plan of action for a business to ensure the achievement of its objectives.

Capital: equipment, machinery, and money.

Capital asset: a long-term asset that is not bought and sold in the ordinary course of business.

Capital requirement: the amount of money required to establish a business or fund a project.

Capital stock: the shares of the owners of a corporation.

Cartel: an association of firms whose purpose is to control the market for a particular product.

Cash basis: a system in which income and expenses are recognized only at the time when cash is received or paid out.

Cash discount: an incentive offered by a seller to a buyer that reduces the amount that the buyer has to pay.

Cash flow: the actual flow of dollars into or out of a business.

Certified cheque: a cheque that is guaranteed by a bank as to signature and adequacy of funds.

Chattel mortgage: a mortgage on personal property other than real estate.

Collateral: security of some sort given to a creditor to guarantee payment.

Collective agreement: an agreement between a union and an employer regarding wages and salaries and other terms of employment.

Common stock: ownership shares in a corporation. Common stock holders are the last to receive any distributions of earnings.

Competition: a situation in which rival firms (sellers) vie for extra business at the expense of one another.

Consignment: an arrangement in which goods are left with a third party for sale. The owner is paid when to goods are sold, and the third party receives the amount agreed upon.

Consumer credit: credit extended to consumers to encourage sales.

Cooperative: a form of business organization owned by its members in which profits are distributed according to patronage.

Corporation: a form of business organization in which shareholders have limited liability. The corporation has the power to act as an individual.

Cost-benefit analysis: the process of weighing and comparing the costs and benefits of a project to aid in the decision making process.

Credit: the ability to obtain goods/services with a promise to pay later.

Creditor: person or organization that has lent money.

Current assets: assets that can be converted to cash within a relatively short time.

Current liabilities: a debt that is expected to be paid within a relatively short time.

Current ratio: the ratio of total current assets to total current liabilities. It is a measure of liquidity.

Dead stock: inventory whose demand has fallen to almost zero.

Debenture bonds: bonds secured by the creditworthiness of the borrower.

Debit: an accounting entry causing an increase in an asset or a decrease in a liability.

Default: failure to meet an obligation at a stipulated time.

Direct costs: expenses that can be directly identified. Direct outlays such as material and labour costs.

Disposable income: personal income remaining after all taxes have been paid.

Diversification: producing or carrying a wide variety of products or engaging in many different business activities.

Dividend: the part of a corporation's profit that is to be paid out to its shareholders.

Entrepreneur: one who organizes a business enterprise and incurs the risks.

Equity: the net worth of a business.

Equity capital: capital acquired from investors without obligation to repay. The investors accept shares in the business.

Exchange rate: the rate at which one country's currency exchanges for that of another.

Feasibility study: a study designed to determine whether an idea or a business has a good chance of success.

Fiscal year: the 12-month period used by a business to indicate its year.

Fixed assets: assets of a business such as buildings, machinery, and equipment that are expected to last for a long time and that will not be converted into cash within a year.

Fixed costs: these are costs that do not change as the volume of production changes. Salaries and rent are examples.

Fixed liabilities: debts that are not due for a least a year.

Franchise: an exclusive right given to someone to perform a stipulated business activity in a specified area.

General partnership: an arrangement whereby two or more people agree to engage in business as owners. Each co-owner has unlimited liability.

Goodwill: the difference between that price paid for a going concern and its book value is taken as a measure of goodwill. It is an intangible asset.

Gross domestic product: the market value of all goods ans services produced in a country during a year.

Gross margin: net sales minus cost of goods sold.

Hidden asset: an asset that is carried on the books of a business at much less than its fair market value.

Holding company: a corporation whose purpose is to own the common stocks of other companies.

Horizontal merger: the amalgamation of separate companies engaged in the same business activity.

Implied warrantee: a warrantee that is implied by law, though not explicitly stated.

Income statement: a financial statement showing revenues, expenses, and net income during a period of time.

Industrial goods: products used by businesses in manufacturing other goods.

Inventory: stocks of finished or semi-finished goods.

Investment portfolio: a list of securities owned by an individual.

Job description: a written statement of the duties and responsibilities of an employee.

Job specification: a statement of the personal and other qualifications required to perform a job satisfactorily.

Kiting: a form of financial fraud that involves using checks to access funds that do not exist because the impacted bank accounts do not hold any money.

KYC: abbreviation for "know your client/customer."

Leverage: the use of external funds to earn profits.

Liability: a debt owed by a business enterprise.

Limited liability: a condition whereby an investor is liable only to the extent of his/her investment in the business.

Line of credit: an arrangement between a financial institution and a borrower whereby the borrower can borrow up to a stipulated amount.

Liquid asset: an asset that can be converted into cash without much loss.

Liquidity: the ability to meet upcoming debt obligations.

Market: a meeting point between buyers and sellers.

Marketing: the various activities involved in directing the flow of goods and services from producers or sellers to the final users.

Marketing plan: a detailed plan outlining how the business will use marketing strategy to achieve its objectives.

Market segmentation: dividing a market into different sub-markets or segments that have similar characteristics.

Markup: an amount or percentage added to the cost price to arrive at the selling price.

Mission statement: a statement of the primary purpose for the existence of the business.

Mortgage: a loan secured by property.

Net profit: operating profit minus income taxes.

Net worth: the difference between total assets and total liabilities.

Overhead: all business costs except direct labor and materials.

Owners' equity: assets remaining after all creditors have been paid off.

Partnership: a business formed by two or more persons who agree to be co-owners of the business.

Partnership agreement: an agreement, usually written, detailing the terms under which the partnership will operate.

Preferred stock: a stock that has certain preferences over common stock.

Price lining: the practice of selling a class of merchandise in a limited number of price categories.

Product differentiation: a market situation achieved by making similar products appear to be different.

Promotion: efforts such as advertising and other activities aimed at increasing sales.

Proprietorship: a business owned and operated by a single owner. It is also known as a single or sole proprietorship.

Quick assets: assets that can be readily converted into cash without appreciable loss.

Retailer: a business that buys goods for resale to the ultimate consumer.

Retained earnings: profits that have not been distributed to shareholders, but retained by the company. Also called *undistributed profits.*

Risk: the probability of suffering a loss.

Risk management: taking steps to prevent losses before they occur.

Serial bonds: bonds issued at the same time but with different maturity dates.

Shareholder: the holder of a share certificate certifying part ownership of a corporation. Also called stockholder.

Silent partner: a co-owner of a partnership who takes no active part in managing the business.

Slow asset: an asset that will take a long time to be converted into cash.

Sole proprietorship: see *proprietorship.*

Speculation: the act of buying and selling with the hope of making a profit from changes in prices.

Spot price: the price of goods for immediate delivery.

Stakeholder: anyone who has financial or other interests in a business.

Stockbroker: an agent who buys and sells stocks and bonds.

Stock dividend: a dividend paid in the form of stock.

Subventions: grants and subsidies.

Surtax: a tax imposed over and above the usual tax.

Target market: the section of the total market selected for special attention or treatment.

Target pricing: a pricing technique designed to produce a 'target' rate of return. Also called *target-return pricing*.

Tax avoidance: legal means of avoiding taxes.

Tax evasion: illegal means of avoiding taxes.

Trade credit: debt arising from credit sales between firms.

Trademark: a distinctive sign or mark that readily identifies a company or its products.

Undercapitalized: with insufficient funds to carry on the current scale of operation.

Undistributed profits: see *retained earnings*.

Union: an organization formed to protect the interest of its members.

Union label: a label indicating that the product was made with unionized labor.

Unlimited liability: a condition whereby a person is fully liable for all debts incurred by his/her business, even to the extent of personal belongings.

Variable costs: costs that vary with the volume of goods produced. They include items such as labor and materials.

Venture capital: an external source of financing for business ventures.

Voting stock: a stock that gives the owner the right to vote at corporate meetings.

Voucher: a document showing that a certain payment is in order and has been authorized.

Warranty: a promise by a seller that the good or service will fulfil a stated requirement during a stipulated time period.

Wholesaler: a middle-person who buys merchandise for resale to retailers and other merchants.

Working capital (net): the difference between current assets and current liabilities.